ITALIANS IN WINNIPEG

ITALIANS IN WINNIPEG

AN ILLUSTRATED HISTORY BY

STANISLAO CARBONE

UNIVERSITY OF MANITOBA PRESS

The University of Manitoba Press
Winnipeg, Manitoba Canada R3T 5V6
www.umanitoba.ca/uofmpress

Printed in Canada

Design: Doowah Design Inc.

Canadian Cataloguing in Publication Data
Carbone, Stanislao, 1957–
Italians in Winnipeg : an illustrated history
ISBN 0-88755-652-3

1. Italians--Manitoba--Winnipeg--History.
2. Italian Canadians--Manitoba--Winnipeg--History.
I. Title.

FC3396.9.I8 C37 1998 971.27'4300451 C98-920208-9
F1065.I8 C37 1998

The University of Manitoba Press gratefully acknowledges the support for its publishing program provided by the Canada Council for the Arts, the Manitoba Arts Council, the Department of Canadian Heritage and the Manitoba Department of Culture, Heritage and Citizenship.

Special assistance for this book has been provided by the Manitoba Italian Heritage Committee.

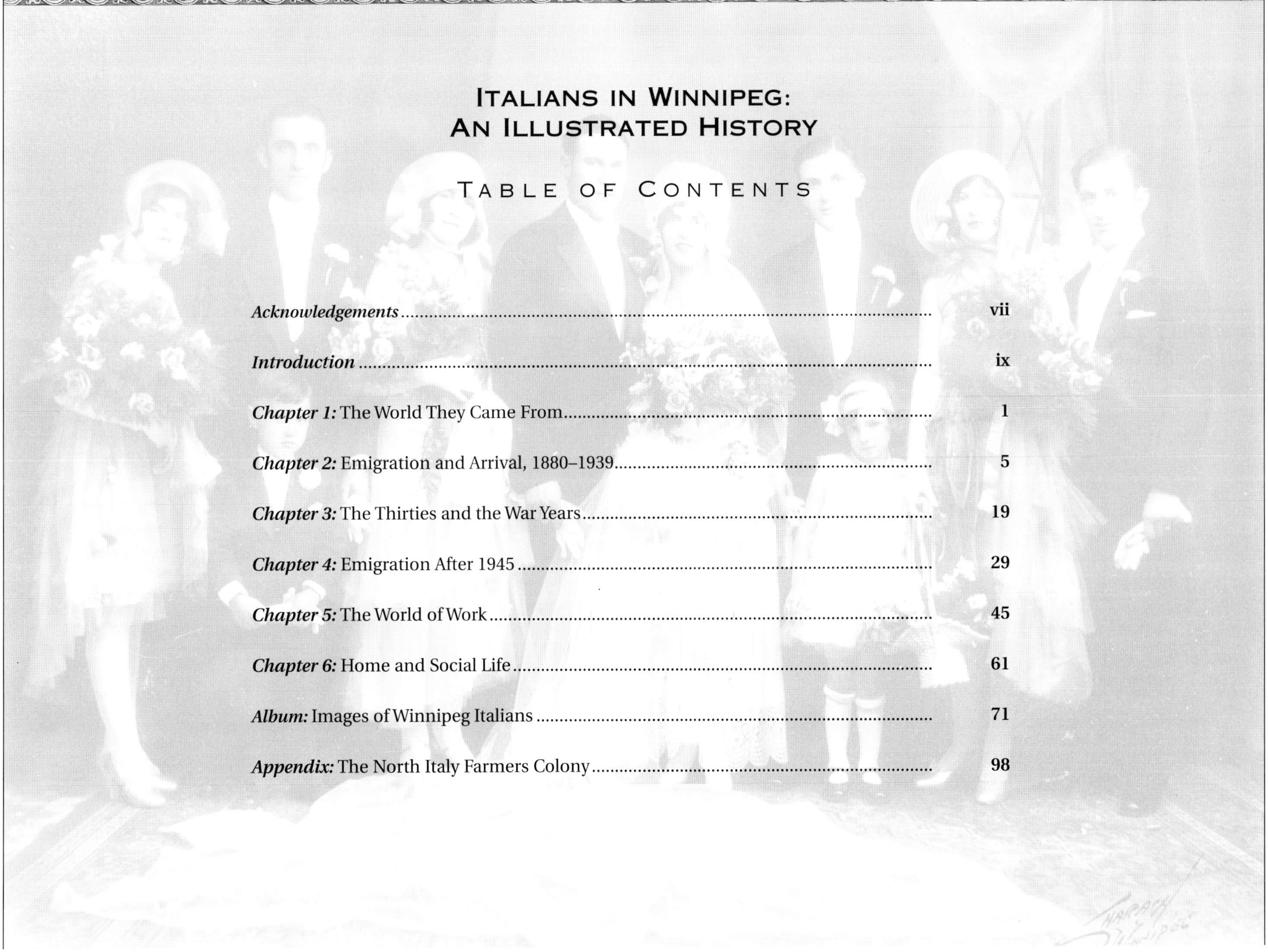

Italians in Winnipeg: An Illustrated History

Table of Contents

Acknowledgements vii

Introduction ix

Chapter 1: The World They Came From 1

Chapter 2: Emigration and Arrival, 1880–1939 5

Chapter 3: The Thirties and the War Years 19

Chapter 4: Emigration After 1945 29

Chapter 5: The World of Work 45

Chapter 6: Home and Social Life 61

Album: Images of Winnipeg Italians 71

Appendix: The North Italy Farmers Colony 98

For Anna

ACKNOWLEDGEMENTS

This publication is a product of the work, dedication and enthusiasm of many individuals and organizations.

The principal organizations involved were the Manitoba Italian Heritage Committee and the University of Manitoba Press. The Committee, which consists of Erminio Caligiuri, Saveria Torquato (who kindly translated the written Italian stories into English), Mario Audino, Angela Luverà-Rattray, Tony De Luca and Dr. Sam Loschiavo, provided the co-ordination and advice needed to carry out the research phase.

At the University of Manitoba Press, I would like to thank David Carr, Allison Campbell, Carol Dahlstrom and Marilyn Morton. Designer Steven Rosenberg of Doowah Design helped to make this book a reality.

The staffs of the University of Manitoba Archives, the University of Winnipeg Library, Provincial Archives of Manitoba, the Manitoba Museum of Man and Nature, the Western Canada Pictorial Index, the National Archives in Ottawa and the Museo Demologico of San Giovanni in Fiore, Italy, went beyond the call of duty in responding to my many requests. The pastors and staff of Holy Rosary Church provided access to valuable documents and photographs.

Funding for the research phase was made possible by a grant from the Manitoba Heritage Grants Advisory Council.

A heartfelt gratitude goes to those individuals who provided the wonderful stories that are critical to the spirit and intent of this publication: Erminio Caligiuri, Teresa Campanelli, my father Rocco Carbone (who interviewed Antonio Paletta), my mother Vittoria Carbone, Giuseppe Colosimo, Leo Copetti, Sonya Dale, Josephine Dellapenta, Adriana De Luca, Gildetta Esposito, Sam Fabro, the Fratellanza Amatese (which conducted an oral history project in 1989 and 1990 and from which I have drawn on August Cosentino's interview of Tommaso Romeo, and Rosina Sinopoli's interviews of Dr. Sam Loschiavo and Annette Stern), Adriana Lombardini, Sam Loschiavo, Francesca Marineo, Pietro Maruca, Teresa Melillo, Matteo Moraca, Diana Nixon, Paolo Nucci, Pat Olsen, Federico Papetti, Marietta Pellettieri, Victor Pucci, Michele Rutigliano, Connie Fiorentino-Scerbo, Charles Sherbo, Giuseppe Torchia, and Victor Venier.

The photographs from families and individuals offer a rich, vibrant and textured visual testimony of the social, cultural and political dimensions which define the history of Italians in Winnipeg. I would like to thank the following for making them available: Teresa Albi, Emilio Anselmo, Josie Audino, Teresa Campanelli, Vittoria Carbone, Leo Copetti, Virginia Cosentino, Sonya Dale, Phil Del Bigio, Henry Dellapenta, Josephine Dellapenta, Vincenza Ens, Gildetta Esposito, Sam Fabro, Cliff Gardner, Marilouise Lisi, Dr. Sam Loschiavo, Guerino Macario, John and Antoinette Mainella, Pietro Maruca, Teresa Melillo, Viera Paletta-Militano, Matteo Moraca, Lucy Mottola, Diana Nixon, Paolo Nucci, Federico Papetti, Marietta Pellettieri, Victor Pucci, Carolina Romeo, Connie Fiorentino-Scerbo, Charles Sherbo, Caterina Bueti-Sotiriadis,

Giuseppe Torchia, and Victor Venier. I also had in my possession reproductions of original photographs from two individuals who are no longer with us, Frank Albi Sr. and Jenny Cascisa.

Some of the individuals whose stories constitute that indispensable human element to the twists and turns of history are no longer with us. I want to pay tribute to those who I knew personally.

Charlie Mazzone, who died in 1992, was the proprietor of the Rancho Don Carlos (first known as Casino Don Carlos), for years Winnipeg's most important night club. When I interviewed Charlie in 1986 he had already reached his eightieth birthday, but he displayed the alertness, astuteness and vitality that obviously served him well in his days at the Rancho.

Tommaso (Tom) Romeo died a few short months before this book went to press. I had the privilege of interviewing Tom several years ago for a video history project on Winnipeg Italians. I will always remember his enthusiasm and pleasing disposition, but more importantly the honesty and courage he displayed when reflecting on the sensitive and emotionally charged topic of the treatment of Italians as enemy aliens during World War II.

Antonio Paletta also passed away shortly before this book saw the light of day. It is difficult to put into words what he meant to my family and me. He was *paesano*, friend, moral supporter, and intellectual stimulus. Antonio's belief in the supremacy of the human spirit, his commitment to social justice and the causes of the less privileged, his respect for nature, his inquisitive mind, and his unwavering commitment to the principles of fraternity and equality were an inspiration to all those who were fortunate enough to have known him. I will always treasure his memory.

My wife Anna, my parents Rocco and Vittoria, and my sister Cathy and her family are a constant source of inspiration. They are integral to my social and cultural identity and have contributed enormously to my awareness of the importance of history. I hope that I have been as integral to their lives.

Identity is the motif which runs through the many social forces that have shaped the formation of an Italian Canadian culture. The most significant of these are social class, gender, family and kinship ties, and ethnicity. Because my identity has been shaped by these forces, I saw my role in the realization of this publication as interpreter of the changing beliefs and traditions of a people and a culture that is constantly redefining itself. I have tried to do justice to their history and to the legacy that they have bequeathed to future generations. It is up to the reader to decide if I have succeeded.

Stanislao Carbone

INTRODUCTION

This book attempts to describe and define the Italian-Canadian experience in Winnipeg. It does this by integrating interpretive text with stories and images in the context of major themes and social forces: emigration and arrival; settlement patterns; work; the Great Depression and World War II; and organizational life. In so doing it becomes a public testament to the contributions that Italian Canadians have made to the social, cultural, and economic development of Winnipeg and how the traditions, beliefs, and mores they brought with them have adapted and modified to life in Canada.

The idea for a history of Winnipeg's Italian community first grew out of the work of the Manitoba Italian Heritage Committee. In 1993, the Committee asked members of the community to come forward with family histories, photographs and other mementos that could be the basis of a collection on the history of Italians in Winnipeg. Over the next several years, more than forty families and individuals provided material that would eventually become the core of this book. Several of the excerpts from oral histories published here also came from interviews conducted in the community by Gabriel Markiw, Rocco Carbone, August Cosentino, Rosina Sinopoli and myself.

The major protagonists of this book are those individuals and families who provided the wonderful stories and photographs that add texture and complexity to the historical drama that is emigration and settlement. In these stories, reason and imagination, memory and reflection, the conscious and subconscious, are woven together to construct the details and experiences of everyday life. The emotions evoked, the sentiments expressed, and the reasoning behind the episodes and nuances described are part of an attempt to provide meaning and purpose to their lives. In the process, the reader is invited to partake in this human journey and share in the agonizing choice to leave the familiarity of one's home town and family for an unknown destination, the emotionally debilitating aspects of solitude in a new land, amazement at the vast expanse of the country, facing a hostile climate and worse yet a hostile population, straining to make sense of the incoherent sounds of a strange language, coming to grips with the idiosyncrasies of new cultural habits, the experience of working under the most difficult of conditions, and the strength and determination to carve out a new life.

From this tapestry of words and images emerges a vibrant collective memory replete with irony, ambiguity, and juxtaposition—where the past, no longer remote or forbidding, becomes both an instrument of community empowerment and a vehicle for enhancing the richness and breadth of Canadian social history by incorporating the Winnipeg Italian experience.

Italian wedding party, 1914 (John and Antoinette Mainella)

Chapter 1

The World They Came From

The Italian immigrants who came to Winnipeg before World War I were mostly *contadini* and *braccianti* (peasants and agricultural labourers) from the towns of Amato and Grimaldi (Calabria), Termini Imerese (Sicily), Campochiaro and Civita di Boiano (Molise), and Azzano Decimo, Sedegliano, and San Daniele (Friuli). They brought with them only vague sentiments of *Italianità* (sense of national pride). They were also a small part of the massive wave of emigration from Italy that had its roots in the disruptions and inequities of nineteenth-century Italian society.

A FAMILY IN AMATO, 1928

For many Italians of this generation, allegiance to the home town–*campanilismo*–was often stronger than their sense as Italians. This was particularly true for those who came from rural areas where the old feudal relations were never properly replaced by market capitalism. In many areas of the *Mezzogiorno* (portions of central and all of southern Italy, including Sardinia), and northeastern Italy, particularly the Friuli region, feudal social relations based on an agrarian economy remained strong.

In the period after Italian unification in 1870, the dichotomy between feudalism and the emerging industrial capitalism was to wreak havoc on Italian society. This tension helped to foster the conditions that brought about the mass emigration from Italy between 1890 and the 1920s.

The towns of origin of many Winnipeg Italians (map: Weldon Hiebert)

The *latifondo* (big landed estate) dominated life in southern Italy. It prevailed because the barons forcibly instituted a series of enclosures that whittled away at common ownership. Co-existing with the *latifondo* was the small peasant landholding. The produce from these parcels of land was so meagre that few peasant families could survive unless they were willing to sell their labour power for regular periods during the year. Many were compelled to work as *braccianti* on the *latifondo*, or, as in Sicily, in the sulphur mines.

The brutal conditions that prevailed throughout the south were described in stark, realistic terms by Robert Foerster:

On the continent married women engage in exhausting toil with deplorable consequences; in Sicily, particularly in the interior, a happier age-old tradition has made for the circumscription of women's labour in the fields. Soon after the age of fourteen, boys undertake the work of men, but the bodies are still unfit for it. Savings are few, a trail of debt common. Often only the clothes on the labourer's back are his own, and in the winter he may verge on starvation. Dire misery has been the lot of the labourers whose strength has left them. Only recently, in Sicily, has it ceased to be common for them to sell their sons into a kind of slavery in the sulphur mines, receiving from the piccioniere, at no interest, a sum of 100–200 lire, while the half-naked boys spent their days carrying heavy loads from the mine's depths to the surface, doomed to baneful toil until the loan should be repaid.[1]

In the 1870s a parliamentary inquiry revealed just how tragic living conditions were in many parts of Italy. From its description of the malaria-infested areas of the south to the pellagra-ridden population of the north-east, the inquiry generated passionate debates. It also brought to the open the problems of child labour, illiteracy, and deplorable housing conditions.

The inquiry took place in the thick of a serious agricultural crisis, exacerbated by the importation of vast quantities of cheap grain and corn from the United States and Russia. Natural disasters also weighed heavily on this state of affairs. In the late 1880s the dreaded disease phylloxera destroyed many vineyards. On top of this, the peasantry was buried under an avalanche of taxes such as the *macinato* (grist mill tax) and the *focatico* (hearth tax).

The peasant who was also a *bracciante*, or who worked in the sulphur mines, was clearly living in a state of economic transition. The old order had not completely died, yet the new order was too weak to replace it. The persistence of feudal relations ensured that the village or *paese* would remain the focus of allegiance for most peasants. Great distances, compounded by poor transportation routes and inadequate means of communication, contributed to this situation. The spirit of *campanilismo* was to maintain a strong hold even in the industrial cauldron of North America.

The *paese* (town or village) was an ensemble of social relations based on class and gender. It was a microcosm of a society that was laboriously entering the world of industrial capitalism. The life of the *paese* depended almost exclusively on one institution: the family. "La Famiglia," as one author put it, "was the centre of Italian life. Families were not only biological arrangements facilitating procreation and socialization but society's basic mode of economic organization in the pre-industrial land."[2]

Emigration was one of the many arrangements that men and women made to cope with the economic and social dilemmas that besieged them. They had to *arrangiarsi*, which meant to devise a pragmatic approach to alleviating their socio-economic woes. *Arrangiarsi* was an integral aspect of the peasant's world view. By understanding this, it will render it less difficult to ascertain the factors that changed emigration from a ripple in the 1870s to the tidal wave it became at the end of the nineteenth century.

Not all chose to emigrate. Some remained and passively accepted their "fate in life." Others joined political movements of the left, which, following unification, were beginning to make their presence felt. In the south more primitive forms of protest, such as anarchism, banditry, and brigandage, took root. Brigandage was particularly evident in regions such as the Basilicata and Calabria. Brigandage could not withstand the winds of change, and it had all but disappeared by the early 1890s when more modern forms of political and economic protest (labour unions, political parties) prevailed.

By the early 1880s, emigration began to reach impressive proportions. Emigration elicited a variety of responses from the Italian ruling class and intelligentsia. For many it was an embarrassment which did little to enhance Italy's aspiration as a colonial power.

While Italian intellectuals and politicians wrote and debated about emigration, millions of Italians, with virtually empty pockets but tremendous inner resolve and an abundance of moral fortitude–attributes that were integral elements of *arrangiarsi*-accepted emigration as a means to preserve their pride and dignity.

The pragmatic considerations to improve one's economic and moral existence created in the swirling dialectical changes of Italian society prepared the emigrant for life in Canada. *Arrangiarsi* manifested itself in the New World in accordance with individual and collective needs. Those who were bent on returning home as soon as possible honed skills that were necessary for a brief sojourning campaign. For those who decided to settle permanently in Canada, *arrangiarsi* meant creatively incorporating new values and practices. Within this context it may have meant a bold leap from industrial proletariat to petty entrepreneurship. It also crystallized through the formation of mutual-aid societies, religious organizations, and sports clubs, all of which played important roles in linking the immigrant to the society at large, provided for financial needs, satisfied the quest for camaraderie, and served as vehicles for the discussion and resolution of individual and collective concerns.

Notes

1. Robert Foerster, *The Italian Emigration of Our Times* (Cambridge: Harvard University Press, 1924), pp. 85–86.
2. John Bodnar quoting Rudolph Bell in *The Transplanted: A History of Immigrants in Urban America* (Bloomington: Indiana University Press, 1987), p. 38.

Roma Society Red Cross Ball, Winnipeg, 1916. (Holy Rosary Church Archives)

CHAPTER 2

Emigration and Arrival 1880 to 1939

From the 1880s to the 1920s, a great wave of emigrants left Italy. Between 1886 and 1890 an average of 222,000 Italians were leaving on an annual basis.[1] From 1896 to 1900, the average annual number grew to 310,435. In just one year (1913), 872,000 Italians left for new homes.[2]

Few of these emigrants, however, were destined for Canada. Canada did not figure prominently in the emigration policies of the Italian government nor did it capture the imaginations of prospective emigrants. Other overseas nations such as Argentina, Brazil, and the United States loomed larger as places of destination.

Before the turn of the century, sporadic attempts had been made to promote the virtues of settling in Canada. In 1881, Egisto Rossi, who would later serve as an immigration agent for the Commissariato Generale dell'Emigrazione (Italian government department of emigration), noted that Canada was in need of good farmers to cultivate land which was "fertile and particularly adaptable to the production of grain."[3] Pietro Pisani, a priest who had travelled throughout North

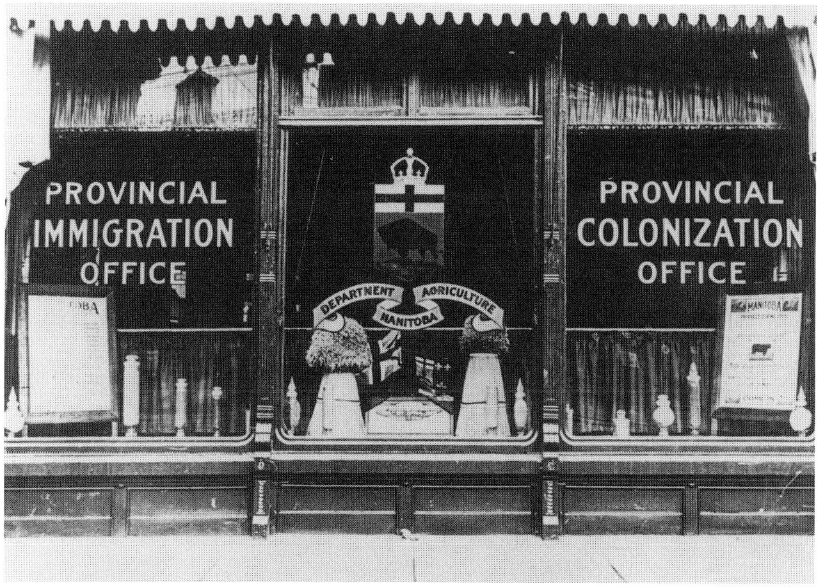

PROVINCIAL IMMIGRATION AND COLONIZATION OFFICE, WINNIPEG, EARLY 1900S.
(PROVINCIAL ARCHIVES OF MANITOBA)

EMIGRANTS EMBARKING ON A TRANSATLANTIC SHIP (PROVINCIAL ARCHIVES OF MANITOBA)

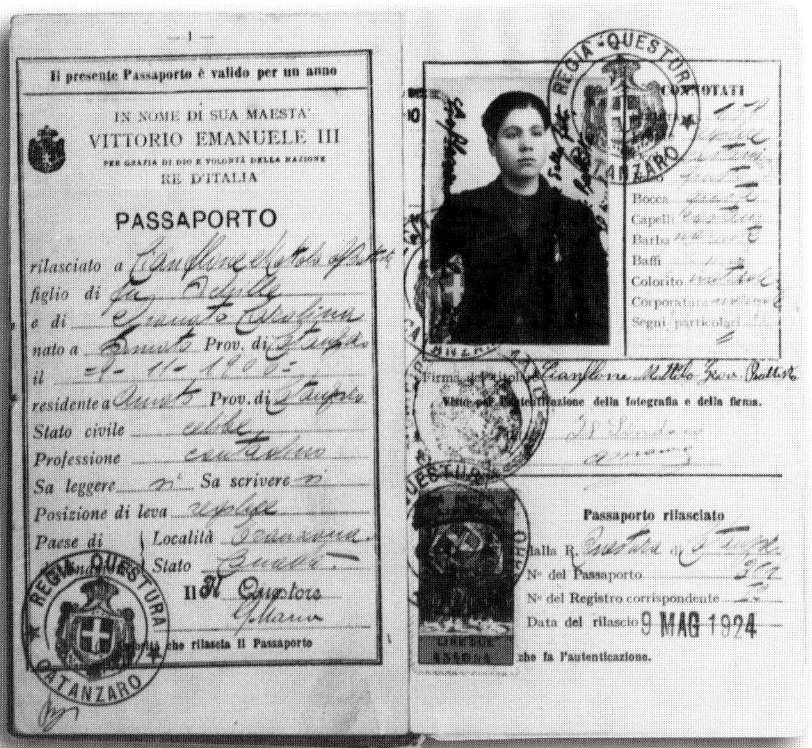

PASSPORT ISSUED TO GIOVANBATTISTA MOTTOLA, 1924 (LUCY MOTTOLA)

America, was of the opinion that "agricultural colonization" would serve a purposeful endeavour for Italians wishing to emigrate. Pisani was particularly enthralled with the Canadian West and cited Manitoba as an ideal place for settlement.

At the time in which Pisani made his comments, the immigration policy of Wilfrid Laurier's government encouraged the settlement of the West. Clifford Sifton, minister responsible for immigration from 1896 to 1905, worked incessantly to populate the Canadian West with individuals who could withstand the severe winters and were willing to roll up their sleeves and administer to the land. Immigrants were also needed because they constituted a workforce that was both cheap and readily

BADALI BROTHERS FRUIT STORE, PORTAGE AND SMITH, WINNIPEG, C.1910. (SENA BADALI)

available for Canada's expanding industries and for projects like the expansion of the western railroads, although the government viewed the development of agriculture as a priority.

Canada's immigration policy in these years favoured emigrants from northern Europe–people who Sifton and others felt were of the right "moral stock" and resolve. Italians, other southern Europeans and Asians were not considered "fit." The Winnipeg Commissioner of Immigration was able to write, without fear of contradiction, that "it is well known that such men as Italians, Assyrians, Jews and Chinese will not make farmers."[4] Sifton even wrote his deputy minister with this blunt order: "I have explained at least a dozen times that I don't want anything done to facilitate Italian immigration."[5]

Italians who did come to Canada were subjected to the scorn and condescending behaviour of Canadian nativists. W.F. McCreary, Divisional Commissioner of Immigration, informed Andrew Blair, Minister of Railways and Canals, that the Canadian Pacific Railways employed "Italians and other foreigners, who, after coming into the country and getting their wages, immediately left it, and were of no great service to the country at large."[6] In 1901, J. Obed Smith, Divisional Commissioner of Immigration in Winnipeg, described Italians as "difficult people to handle" and feared that "this class of immigration will not do our country any good."[7] James A. Smart, the Deputy Minister of the Interior wrote to a Presbyterian minister that "Italians generally speaking, will make very poor

DOMINION IMMIGRATION BUILDING, WINNIPEG, C. 1904. (PROVINCIAL ARCHIVES OF MANITOBA)

settlers on the land." By contrast,

while some people may not regard the Scotch altogether as the 'salt of the earth', yet we must admit, our forefathers have perhaps made more headway than any other nationality, in whatever they have undertaken not only in Canada but elsewhere.[8]

Those Italians who came to Canada at the turn of the century were peasants, artisans and agricultural labourers who largely settled in the expanding cities of central Canada, especially Montreal and Toronto. There they worked as factory and construction workers, food and fruit merchants, building contractors or artisans. Italians started to arrive in Winnipeg in the late 1870s. By 1901 there were 147 people of Italian origin residing in Winnipeg. That would increase to 769 in 1911, 1,311 in 1921, and 1,664 by 1941. The censuses of 1911 and 1921 showed that two-thirds of these were men. In 1913, however, the *Manitoba Free Press* reported that the ratio of men to women among Italians in Winnipeg was as high as seven to one.[9]

Before 1914, people from the town of Termini Imerese (Sicily) constituted the largest segment of the Italian population in Winnipeg. The people of Amato (Calabria) were also a strong numerical

ITALIAN RAILWAY WORKERS AT THE FORT ROUGE CNR SHOPS, WINNIPEG, C.1928. (LUCY MOTTOLA)

force. In fact, by the early 1920s the Amatesi had supplanted the Termitani as the principal subgroup of Winnipeg Italians. In addition there were immigrants from the towns of Grimaldi (also in Calabria), Campochiaro and Civita di Boiano (Molise), and Azzano Decimo, Sedegliano and San Daniele (Friuli).

Winnipeg profited enormously from immigrant labour. The city achieved economic growth as a result of its development into a major centre for grain production and distribution and because it emerged as the most important railway terminus north of Chicago. In 1901, Winnipeg's population was 42,000; by 1913 it had tripled to 150,000. It became the West's most important commercial centre, earning such nicknames as the "Gateway to the West" and the "Chicago of the North."

Winnipeg Italians had similar occupations to their counterparts in central Canada. Some Italians also went into farming, which was in contradiction to the views expressed by McCreary and other government bureaucrats. By the 1920s a cooperative farming venture known as the North Italy Farmers Colony, consisting largely of settlers from the Lomellina district in Lombardy, had purchased acres of land south of Winnipeg, near Lorette, near Alonsa and in the Glenella district. By the late 1920s, however, the Colony had dissolved (see Appendix for more details).

In the 1920s and the 1930s Italian immigration to Winnipeg and to Canada diminished greatly, largely due to two factors: the advent of Fascism in Italy and the Great Depression. The Fascist regime which took power in 1922 began to reduce the flow of labour out of Italy. By the late 1930s many Italians who might have emigrated to North America went instead to the settlements in Italy's new colonial possessions of Ethiopia, Somalia, and Libya. At the same time, as a result of the Depression the Canadian government greatly restricted the flow of new immigrants. By the 1930s, arrivals had dropped off to an all-time low, and for the first time in four decades more people actually left Canada than came to it.

Notes

1. Giuliano Procacci, *History of the Italian People* (Harmondsworth: Penguin Books, 1968), p. 343.
2. A. M. Ratti, "Migratorie, Correnti," in *Enciclopedia Treccani*, vol. 23 (1934, 1949) pp. 256–57.
3. John Zucchi, *Italians in Toronto: Development of a National Identity 1875–1935* (Montreal: McGill-Queen's University Press, 1988), p. 18.
4. Letter from W. F. McCreary, Commissioner of Immigration in Winnipeg to the Hon. Andrew G. Blair, Minister of Railways and Canals, 21 June 1897.
5. Sifton quoted in D.J.Hall, Clifford Sifton, Vol.2, *A Lonely Eminence* (Vancouver: University of British Columbia Press, 1981–1985),p. 68.
6. W. F. McMreary to Andrew Blair.
7. Letter from J. Obed Smith, Divisional Commissioner of Immigration in Winnipeg, to James A. Smart, Deputy Minister of the Interior, 27 August 1901.
8. Letter from James A. Smart, Deputy Minister of the Interior to Rev. William Patrick of Manitoba College, 27 May 1904.
9. *Manitoba Free Press*, 10 January 1913.

L I F E S T O R I E S

GIOVANBATTISTA MOTTOLA *was born in Amato in 1905, and came to Canada at the age of 18. Many years later, he would act as Italian vice-consul in Winnipeg.*

We sailed from the Port of Palermo in 1924. It took us 14 days before we disembarked at Halifax. The name of the boat was the *Dante Alighieri* and it was crowded. We were in a cabin where there were 28 passengers. We had to wash our own dishes. They gave each passenger a sack full of dishes. You went to the kitchen, which was cafeteria style, and you picked up your food, and after you were finished you went and washed your own dishes in salt water. It wasn't very nice but we had to do that for 14 days. From the ports of landing like Halifax or Montreal to whatever destination you went to like Toronto or Winnipeg you had to sleep in special coaches. You could open them up and sleep on them. They had two seats that were placed together and a wooden bunk which was placed on top.

The thing that I remember vividly about the first years in Canada–and will stay with me for a long time–was the loneliness. It was a very lonely life, because in the first place I couldn't speak the language, and I didn't have much money to spend. In the morning I hated to see the sun come.

TOMMASO ROMEO *was born in Amato in 1905.*

We left from the port of Naples in 1924 on a ship called the *President Wilson*. I was afraid I wasn't going to come out alive. There were 800 people on the ship, and I was sick almost every day. At Naples they put us into this building and asked us to take off our clothes. You would think that we were a bunch of convicts. They fumigated our suits and suitcases. It was like being in a "crazy house." When we got out we were exhausted. Then we were led through a small passage just like cattle. They gave us a book to see if we could read. I never expected that. Quite a few could not pass the reading test. Twenty-two days on the ship was too long. When we passed Gibraltar we went through some rough waters.

We docked at New York and from there went to Chicago and then crossed the border to Fort Frances, Ontario where we took a CN train to Winnipeg. In Winnipeg we were greeted by my brother, and my *paesani* Saverio Fiorentino and Michele Cantafio.

Soon after, I found work at the Fort Rouge CNR shops. There were a lot of *paesani* working at the shops. We used to work on the boxcars. We would take out the wood and leave the frame. Our boss, Jimmy Mazzone, would sell the wood to the public. Many Italians would use the wood to build their homes. You have to give the Italians credit, they always wanted to progress.

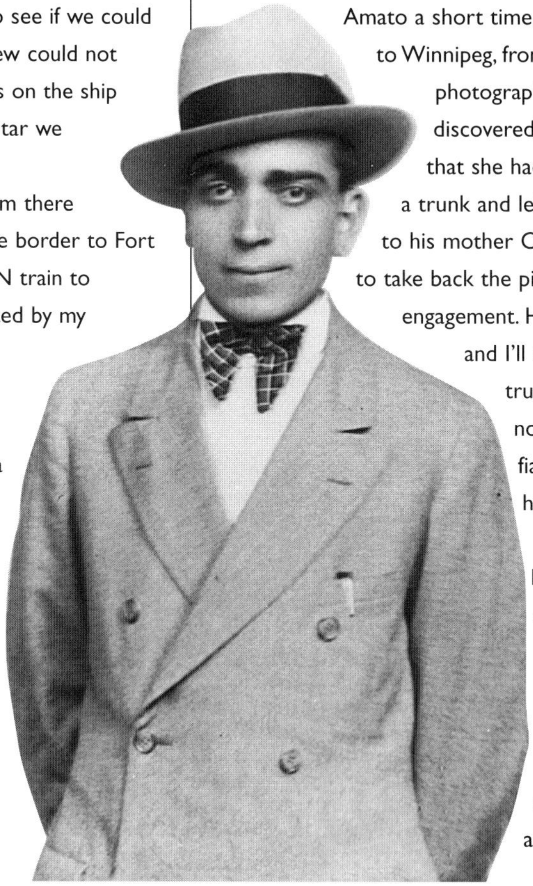

TOMMASO ROMEO, 1930.

ARCANGELO SHERBO *was born in Amato in 1877. He made his first trip to Canada at the age of 14, and would cross the Atlantic eight more times over the next 35 years. His story is told by his grandson Charles Sherbo.*

My grandfather left Italy in 1891 at the age of 14. He travelled by ship across the Atlantic, and then by train to Winnipeg. In 1891, he was one of a few Italians, and possibly the first Amatese, in Winnipeg. He began working as a railroad water boy for a few years, and then returned to Amato to be engaged. He stayed in Amato a short time, and then went back to Winnipeg, from where he sent his photograph to his fiancée. He discovered a short time later that she had put his picture into a trunk and left it there. He wrote to his mother Carmela, and asked her to take back the picture and to end the engagement. He said, "I need air, and I'll choke if I stay in a trunk." Perhaps he had a notion of what his fiancée would be like as his wife for a lifetime! Carmela wrote back and said she had selected another girl for him, but this girl was still very young. At his mother's request he returned once more to Amato, and met Maria Anania.

She was an orphan, who had been raised by her uncle Antonio Anania. My grandfather agreed to delay the wedding until she was older, and he again returned to Winnipeg, and to his hard life as a railway worker. In 1908, he crossed the Atlantic for the sixth time, to marry Maria in Amato. She was 15 years old, and he was 32.

The newlyweds built a house, and intended to remain in Amato. Eventually their plans changed because they wanted to have children and provide them with greater opportunities. In 1912, they came to Winnipeg while they were expecting their first child. Carmelina was born in Winnipeg, and over the next seven years the couple had four more children.

Despite the initial promise, their life in Winnipeg was very difficult, and Maria was not in good health after giving birth to five children, and suffering a number of miscarriages. In 1921, parents and children returned to Amato. The ship carrying Arcangelo's family passed a ship which carried Francesco Maruca, also of Amato, who was travelling across the Atlantic to live in Winnipeg; he later married Angelarosa (Arcangelo's daughter), in 1934.

ARCANGELO AND MARIA SHERBO IN FRONT OF HOLY ROSARY CHURCH, WINNIPEG, 1947. (CHARLES SHERBO)

The family remained in Amato, and lived in the house which had been built more than a decade earlier. They intended to remain in Amato, but that resolve did not last in Calabria's depressed economy. In 1923, Arcangelo decided to return to Winnipeg. This was to be his ninth and last Atlantic crossing by boat, and he never returned to his home town. For the time being his family remained in Amato. Maria was pregnant with twins–Sera and Virginia–and was left to raise her family of seven children. Tony was 10 years old, and as the oldest male, took on some responsibility for his siblings.

Arcangelo was determined to establish a life for his family in Winnipeg, but he had to have a source of income and save enough money before he could send for Maria and the children. He worked as a shoemaker in his own shop on Notre Dame Avenue. The small building was in poor shape, and during the frigid Winnipeg winters ice formed on the inside of the walls. He lived in attics of other Italians' homes, or in boarding rooms.

During his time alone in Winnipeg, Arcangelo helped other Italians by writing to their families in Italy, because he was one of the few at the time who were literate. He worked hard, did without many necessities, and indulged in no luxuries.

In Canada during the 1920s immigrants did well not to stand apart from the Anglo-Saxon majority. In order to assimilate in his new home, Arcangelo changed the spelling of his family name from Scerbo to "Sherbo" so it would sound as it was spelled in English.

He also became a Canadian citizen, to cement his commitment to the country of his choice.

By 1930, Arcangelo had enough money to rent a house of his own, and he sent for his family. The family left from the port of Naples–all, that is, except for the eldest, Carmelina, who stayed with her new husband (she later emigrated to Winnipeg in January 1949; when she walked up to the family home on Stradbrook, she picked up a handful of snow to eat).

On November 3, 1930, the family landed at New York. Young Tony, then only 16 years old, left the group to find the relative of a friend who lived in Brooklyn. He made it back just in time for the train to Winnipeg, but not before causing his mother even more worry than she already faced.

On November 6 (Tony's 17th birthday) Maria and her six children arrived in Winnipeg. The twins, Virginia and Sera, then nine years old, had never seen their father, and they were reticent when they first met him; he was, at times, a stern man. Their first home was a rented house on Kennedy Street, across from the Law Courts Building. The children soon became accustomed to Winnipeg; in winter they slid down the snowy steps of the courthouse on homemade cardboard toboggans.

VIRGINIA COSENTINO, *née Sherbo, was one of the twin girls who came with their mother to Winnipeg in 1930. She remembers that reunion through the eyes of a young child.*

When we left Amato, it was pouring rain. I can still see my grandmother weeping. She remarked, "I'll never see you again." She knew that once we came to Canada we would never return.

We arrived on November 6, and it was very cold. I just didn't know what to expect. I didn't know my father and I was going to meet this man who was *supposedly* my father. It was a bit frightening, but after a few months we had warmed up to him and things worked out fine.

We had come from a town and we arrived in this big city where the homes were heated by furnaces. Before we left for Canada, Mother took us to a dressmaker in Catanzaro, and had us outfitted in silk dresses and satin overcoats. The day after we arrived in Canada, Dad went to the closest department store, which was Eaton's, and had us outfitted in winter clothes; otherwise we couldn't go out. I remember we also had pierced ears. In those days, infants in Italy would often get their ears pierced. Dad immediately had us take our earrings off because most children in Canada didn't wear earrings. He said, "I don't want my children to be different. I want them to fit with the other children."

VIRGINIA (NÉE SHERBO) AND AUGUST COSENTINO, WINNIPEG, 1945. (VIRGINIA COSENTINO)

JOHN BATTISTA AIELLO *was born 1896 in Amato and came to Canada as a young teenager. A few years later, he would return to his homeland with the Canadian army. His story is told by his daughter Diana Nixon.*

My father "Tita" grew up in difficult times. The family decided that he would leave home to follow his older brother Luigi's footsteps to Canada. "Tita" and Luigi would then be able to assist the family by working and sending them money.

He arrived in Canada in 1911 at the age of 15. Upon arrival in Winnipeg he was sent west on a railway section gang working as a waterboy. When he was a little older, he laid tracks for the Grand Trunk and Canadian Northern Railways as far west as Jasper, Alberta.

With the outbreak of World War I in 1914, Battista joined the Canadian army, serving with the 221st Battalion. He was posted to Italy and requested a transfer to the 63rd Regiment of the Italian army. Fighting in northern Italy and almost starving, the regiment had to resort to eating cooked grass and meat from dead horses. One day a surprise visitor boosted the morale of the soldiers. Dressed in fatigues and surrounded by guards, King Vittorio Emanuele III of Italy passed out cigarettes, chocolates, and words of encouragement to the men. For Battista, this encounter was one of the highlights of his life.

During intense fighting, a grenade virtually wiped out the whole regiment, leaving Battista as the sole survivor. He was captured by the German army and remained a prisoner of war for almost a year. Battista picked up enough German and Polish in the camps to enable him to act as an interpreter for the prisoners. In recognition of his bravery, he was decorated with the Italian government's Ordine di Vittorio Veneto. He returned to Winnipeg in 1921, and worked with the CNR Fort Rouge railway shops.

FRANCESCO LOSCHIAVO *came to Winnipeg after two earlier emigrations–first to Brazil in 1898 and then to Panama in 1910, where he worked on the construction of the Panama Canal. He returned to Amato in 1913, but stayed only a few months before leaving for North America. His son, Sam Loschiavo, tells his story.*

THE LOSCHIAVO FAMILY, WINNIPEG, C. 1930.
CATERINA, FRANCESCO, SAM. (SAM LOSCHIAVO)

After leaving Milan en route to America via Switzerland, Dad was asked for his passport. He didn't have one but showed his birth certificate instead. When asked his destination, Dad said Switzerland. He was allowed to remain on the train, but at the border crossing of Chiasso, an agent told Dad that he couldn't go any further without a passport. However, he was told that if he wanted to go to the United States, he could do so without a passport because at that time it wasn't required. The agent then suggested to Dad that if he wanted to go to Canada he could cross over from the United States.

Instead of going into Switzerland Dad made his way to Le Havre, France, and booked passage on the ship *Chicago* destined for New York. Friends in New York informed him that work was scarce there but that there were better opportunities in Canada with its rapidly expanding railway system. Dad knew of friends in Winnipeg so he boarded a train for Chicago, Minneapolis, and Winnipeg. After leaving Minneapolis the train stopped at Emerson. A man in civilian clothes boarded the train and asked Dad how much money he had. Dad told him he had $5. Actually he had $40, but he wasn't going to tell this to a stranger without a uniform. He was asked to take his suitcase and get off the train. Then he was brought into an office in the station, where he was asked by someone in uniform whether he knew anyone in Winnipeg. Dad told him he had an uncle, Gaetano Loschiavo. In fact, he wasn't an uncle at all, but only a distant relative who was not even aware that Dad was coming to Winnipeg. Dad claimed him as an uncle, thinking that naming a close relative would facilitate his entry into Canada. When the newly created "uncle" was contacted he naturally was surprised, and told the official that he was not expecting a nephew from Italy. When the official in Emerson told Dad what his "uncle" had said, Dad probably thought he would be sent back to Italy. In fact, Dad was treated very kindly. The official asked him how much money he had. This time Dad said he had $25 even though he had more. The official tried to explain that with a minimum of $25 Dad could have entered Canada without the need of a sponsor. Dad did not need an "uncle" in Winnipeg. In those days $25 was a considerable sum of money.

The next day, Dad boarded the train bound for Winnipeg. He first realized that he was in Canada when he looked out of the train window and saw a country house with a Union Jack flying over it. He arrived in Winnipeg on May 14, 1914. Dad showed a policeman a paper with Gaetano's address and once again Dad was asked the universal question about money. The policeman called a cab and Dad finally arrived at his "uncle's" shoe shop on Sargent Avenue. The cab driver charged $3 for the short trip. Thus Dad's first financial transaction in Canada was one in which he was taken advantage of.

Dad stayed with Gaetano one night, and next day was taken to a boarding house at the corner of Alexander and Sherbrook where there were many young Italian men seeking work in Canada or already working. The house was owned by an Italian named Joe Scalise. Dad stayed there for just a day and then moved to a house on Pacific Avenue where there were friends from Amato, Francesco Cantafio, Francesco Aiello, and others.

ALFONSINA FILOMENA PERRELLA *was born in 1910 in Monteverde (Molise). When she was an infant, her father, Giuseppe and her uncle, Giocondo, went to South America to work as brickmakers. A few months later, Giuseppe died from a snake bite. When Alfonsina was 11, her mother, Maddalena, married Giocondo, who had returned from South America. Alfonsina's story is told by her daughter Josephine Dellapenta.*

In May of 1921, Alfonsina and her parents left for Canada. First they travelled to Naples by train, where they discovered that there was an error in their travelling documents. They were delayed for six days and missed their ship.

When things were resolved they travelled by train to Belgium, where they had to wait another week to embark on the ship to Canada. Almost everyone waiting for the ship was Polish, and there was only one other woman who could speak Italian. Because of the language problem they could not ask questions. After some difficulties they finally understood that the hotel they were staying in had no more empty rooms. They had to stay in the dining room, sitting on hard straight-backed chairs. They slept in these conditions for three nights.

On the fourth, everyone waiting for the ship was directed to a bathhouse where they had to take a shower. The women and children went to one area, and the men to another. When Alfonsina and her mother were shown to a shower stall they understood that they were to remove their clothing and hand it to a waiting attendant. All of a sudden they felt a spray of water hitting their heads and spilling over their bodies. This came as a sudden shock. Soon their eyes were burning. When their showers were over they were handed towels to dry off. Their clothes, which had been disinfected, were handed to them. Once they were dressed, the children were sent to the fathers, while the mothers were to receive medical checkups. Maddalena saw a doctor who spoke Italian. He asked her why she hadn't changed her clothes, to which she responded that because they were "lodging" in the hotel dining room there was no place to change and had she known that they would be given the opportunity to shower she would have taken clean clothing. The doctor was shocked at these revelations, especially at the fact that they were staying in the dining room. He gave Maddalena a note to relay to the hotel clerk which expressly stated that the family be given a room. Subsequently, the hotel clerk assigned Maddalena and Alfonsina to a room with two other women, and Giocondo to a room with some men.

Crossing the ocean was a traumatic experience. They found the food very difficult to eat, for most of it tasted like iodine. Whenever the sea became rough and stormy the passengers were sent to an area with park-like benches located below the main deck. There everyone would remain until the waters calmed.

Shortly after their arrival in Quebec and prior to leaving the ship, passengers went through a medical inspection. If everything was okay they would receive a green card. If the opposite was the case a passenger could not leave the ship. Once off the ship they went through Immigration. From Immigration Maddalena and the others had to walk two miles (with their belongings) to the train station, where they left for Montreal. In the Montreal train station there was a huge laundry room. Maddalena washed all the family's clothes by hand as there were no machines or scrub boards. To dry the clothes, she hung them over steam-heated radiators.

Two days later they left for Winnipeg where Maddalena had a brother–Francesco Perrella.

Winnipeg was no bed of roses! In addition to not knowing the language, jobs were scarce. Giocondo worked a few mornings a week with the City of Winnipeg, sawing wood which was to be used as firewood. In return he received food stamps. He also went door to door sharpening scissors and knives for a few cents. Maddalena took care of household duties and Alfonsina went to school. Thus they were introduced to the "Canadian way of life," which they found very different-and very difficult.

ANTONIO AND RACHELA TORCHIA ON THEIR 50TH WEDDING ANNIVERSARY, WINNIPEG 1952 (JOE TORCHIA)

Like many immigrants, **ANTONIO TORCHIA** *spent many years alone, working to save enough money to bring his wife and children from Italy. His story is told by his son Giuseppe Torchia.*

My father had spent several years in "America," having gone there before World War I. He returned to Italy to serve in the Italian army from 1915 to 1918.

Before emigrating to "America," Father had been a labourer. Economic conditions were bad, forcing him to leave Italy and come to Canada. First he laid railroad tracks and later worked in the Transcona CNR shops. My father sponsored my brother Gregorio, who came to Winnipeg in 1922. Only when he was able to buy a house did he send for the rest of the family.

My mother, brothers and I (aged nine) sailed from the port of Palermo, Sicily, on board the ship named after Italy's great opera composer, Giuseppe Verdi. Travelling third class, the trip, which was a rough one, took 14 days. I will never forget how those gigantic waves tossed the ship back and forth. We were all seasick. In addition, the ship's engine wasn't working properly. On the other hand, one of the nice things that I remember was when we met the liner Dante Alighieri in mid-ocean. The people on both ships waved to one another.

A funny incident happened while we were playing on deck. My brother Frank, who was two years younger than me, picked up a cigarette butt and placed it in the open mouth of an old lady who had dozed off while on a deck chair. My poor mother had a hard time appeasing the lady's anger.

Another time we were watching people drinking beer at the bar. We had never seen beer before, and the thick foam seemed so desirable that I begged my mother to buy me a glass. She, of course, refused to do so.

We landed at Ellis Island, New York, and made our way to Toronto, where Father was there to meet us. We arrived in Winnipeg (Transcona) on October 1, 1926. My first impression was rather unfavourable. The wooden homes seemed (and were) flimsy in comparison to the solid stone houses in Italy. Also, the streets were largely unpaved. When we arrived the roads were quite muddy. There were no flowers, which were so common back home.

The language was difficult at first, but by going to school and playing with other children, we learned to speak fluently. Our first winter in Canada was severe, especially to us who were accustomed to the beautiful Mediterranean climate. There was so much snow! We used to heat our home with a wood and coal stove, with pipes carrying the heat from room to room. My father would often stay up during the night to keep the fire going.

PIETRO MARUCA *came to Winnipeg as a young boy. His father Antonio had gone ahead of the family to establish a home, so Pietro made the journey with his mother and younger brother.*

It was with mixed emotions that we left Amato, and on July 31, 1925 we left the port of Naples. In our company were Caterina Falvo and her son Joe, and Mrs. Ida Cantafio and daughter Lucia. The voyage was long and the sea was rough. My mother was seasick. At dinner I would yell "Santa Mamma, la campana suona andiamo a mangiare" (Holy Mother, the bell is ringing, let's go and eat). This of course made Mother worse.

We arrived at New York on August 13, 1925. Soon we were separated from our friends. We were to travel on a CPR train, while the Cantafios and the Falvos boarded a CN train. The train came to a stop at the CPR station on Higgins Avenue. Soon we were left all alone in the middle of the station with no one to greet us. My father had been given the wrong time schedule. Mr. Giovanni Fabbri, who owned a grocery store and deli across from the station, came to our rescue. Mother was very happy to hear Italian spoken. She chattered away like a magpie. I was also very happy, eating all the food that was presented to me.

Finally, with the help of Mr. Fabbri we took a taxi and made our way to Transcona through bush and gravel roads, and finally arrived at the Vimy Block, a three-storey building which was to be our new home.

ITALIAN WORKERS ON THE GRAND TRUNK PACIFIC NEAR STRATHCONA, ALBERTA, 1909. L TO R: FRANCESCO FALVO, ANTONIO MARUCA AND GIUSEPPE ROMEO (PETER MARUCA)

Houses were few and far between. When it rained roads were extremely muddy. Sidewalks were made of wood and some were elevated because of the snow thaw in the spring. The winters were very severe and most homes were heated by wood stoves or coal heaters. Many a morning my father would thaw the water pipes to get the water to flow.

My first day at school was quite an experience. Lucy Cantafio took me and introduced me to the principal, who assigned me to a particular classroom. I noticed that some of the kids were putting their hands up and leaving the room. After a while I put up my hand, left the room, and went home. Mother was shocked. I was returned immediately, to the relief of my teacher, and was told that the other children raised their hands because they needed to go to the washroom.

ANNETTE STERN, *née Morello, came to Winnipeg as a young girl.*

My dad must have left Amato when I was six months old. He had returned to Canada in order to make money and send for us. My mother and maternal grandmother looked after us. We had to do the best we could. We had lots of friends and relatives, but it wasn't like having a father. He would keep sending money and photographs.

When we came in 1933 and met him in the railway station, he said to me, "Well, who is this cute little girl?" And I said, "Don't you know? This is the coat you sent me. Can't you tell that it's me?! Your daughter?!"

I never had a normal childhood. At the age of seven, I had to leave Italy to come to Canada. Almost immediately I started assuming a lot of household responsibilities. I was signing legal documents, taking my mom and dad to doctors, lawyers, and dentists, where I had to do all the translating. I don't believe I suffered because of these experiences. I also don't feel too sorry for people that are saying how hard times are today. They should have been around when I was growing up.

The thing that got to me was my first day at school. I saw kids with holes in their clothes and shoes. Some of them had stuffed cardboard in their shoes to cover the holes. I thought to myself: So this is Winnipeg?! Is this the land of plenty? Is this the place which was supposed to have gold on the streets? In Amato we were better dressed, yet these kids had holes in their clothes.

THE MORELLO CHILDREN, WINNIPEG, C. 1940S. L. TO R. ANNETTE, MURRAY AND TERESA. (TERESA ALBI NÉE MORELLO)

Banquet in honor of Holy Rosary Church parishioners who served during the war, 1946. (Holy Rosary Church Archives)

CHAPTER 3

The Thirties and The War Years

The 1930s and 1940s were rife with momentous events and social processes that affected Winnipeg Italians. The Great Depression created financial havoc and great emotional and psychological trauma for many individuals and families whose attempt to create a sense of belonging in Canada was being undermined. The rise and development of Fascism in Italy, the relationship between Catholicism and Fascism, and events prior to and during World War II brought significant challenges and created anxieties and tensions in the moral and social fabric of the Winnipeg Italian community.

Throughout Canada in the 1930s, Italian Catholic parishes in conjunction with local consular agencies played a vital role in promoting Fascism and the principles of *Italianità* (which referred to the "high ideals and splendour" of Italian culture) as defined by official Fascist doctrine. Whereas in major centres such as Toronto and Montreal the Church was one of a variety of organizations that carried out these objectives, in Winnipeg it had a virtual monopoly.

A CHRISTMAS CARD FROM GUS COSENTINO, C. 1943 (LUCY MOTTOLA)

ITALIAN-BELGIAN BANQUET HONORING THE WEDDING OF PRINCE UMBERTO AND PRINCESS MARIE-JOSÉ, WINNIPEG, 1930. (LUCY MOTTOLA)

The most intensive campaign was waged between 1929 and 1933, when Manlio Ciufoletti served as pastor of the Holy Rosary Church. Ciufoletti was an indefatigable and zealous advocate of *Italianità*. For example, in 1929 he was largely responsible for organizing a lavish dinner and ceremony to commemorate, all in one occasion, the signing of the Lateran Treaty, the eleventh anniversary of the Italian armistice, and tributes to King Vittorio Emmanuele III and Prince Umberto. The following year, Ciufoletti helped organize a banquet in honour of the marriage between Prince Umberto and Princess Marie-José of Belgium. Ciufoletti was also responsible for setting up Italian language classes which were conducted in the basement of the Holy Rosary Church. The classes were a main feature of the church's cultural activities until the advent of World War II, when they were banned as a result of Italy's declaration of war on Canada.

One of the language teachers was Angelo Marzola, a real-estate agent and notary public, who was to be appointed consular agent with the backing of Ciufoletti. Marzola's predecessor, Giuseppe Barattieri di San Pietro, was known for his uncompromising antipathy towards Fascism. This irked Ciufoletti considerably. With the assistance of a group of self-professed defenders of *Italianità*, Ciufoletti was able to exert enough pressure on the Italian Ministry of External Affairs (the government department responsible for appointing consular agents) to have Barattieri dismissed from his duties. For a few months in 1930, until Marzola's appointment, Ciufoletti served as acting consular agent.

Ciufoletti left the diocese in 1933. Marzola, who served as vice-consul until 1932, was replaced by Giovanni Binda. In 1935, Binda wholeheartedly supported an initiative by several individuals to collect gold to help finance Italy's invasion of Ethiopia.

Fascism may have been disconcerting to certain sectors of the Canadian society, such as the labour movement, but in some circles of the political and economic elite it met with approval. The Fascist propaganda machine had succeeded in promoting Mussolini as a dynamic individual who had established law and order in a country that only recently was on the verge of succumbing to the wiles of Communism. He especially appealed to those who believed that Fascism would have a civilizing influence on a country "teeming with illiteracy, crime, filth, and other symptoms of a deficient national character."[1]

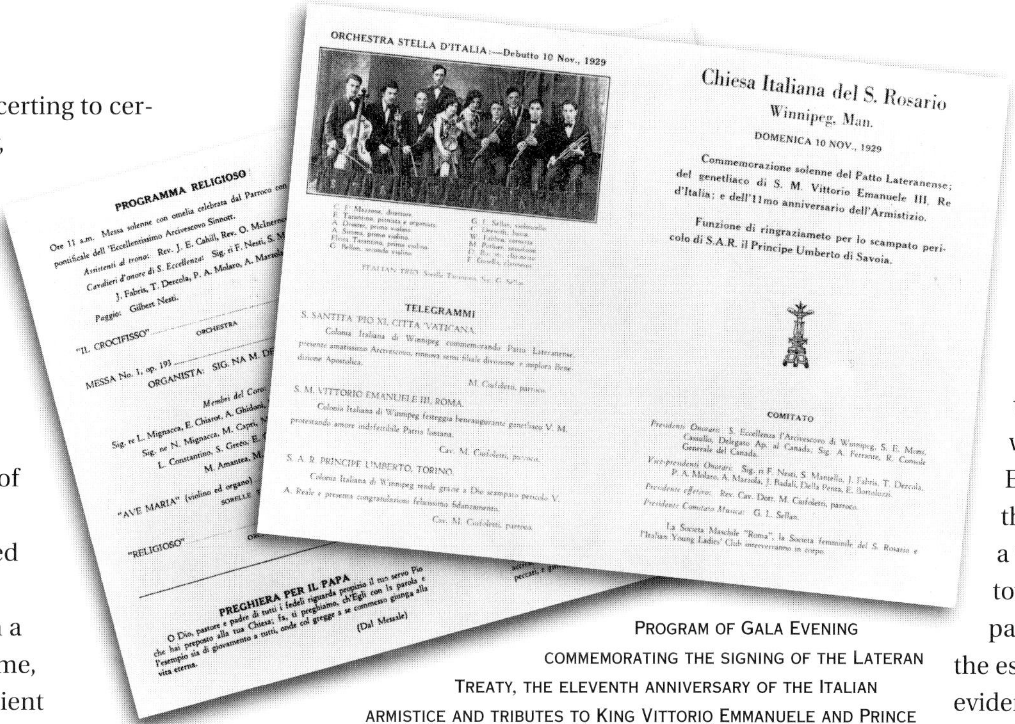
PROGRAMMA RELIGIOSO
Ore 11 a.m. Messa solenne con omelia celebrata dal Parroco con
pontificale dell 'Eccellentissimo Arcivescovo Sinnott.
Assistenti al trono: Rev. J. E. Cahill, Rev. O. McInerne
Cavalieri d'onore di S. Eccellenza: Sig. ri F. Nesti, S. M
J. Fabris, T. Dercola, P. A. Molaro, A. Marzola
Paggio: Gilbert Nesti.
"IL CROCIFISSO" .... ORCHESTRA
MESSA No. 1, op. 193 ....
ORGANISTA: SIG. NA M. DE
Membri del Coro:
Sig. re L. Mignacca, E. Chiarot, A. Ghidoni,
Sig. ne N. Mignacca, M. Capri,
L. Constantino, S. Greco, E.
M. Amantea, M.
"AVE MARIA" (violino ed organo)
SORELLE
"RELIGIOSO" ....
PREGHIERA PER IL PAPA
O Dio, pastore e padre di tutti i fedeli riguarda propizio il tuo servo Pio
che hai preposto alla tua Chiesa; fa, ti preghiamo, ch'Egli con la parola e
l'esempio sia di giovamento a tutti, onde col gregge a se commesso giunga alla
vita eterna.
(Dal Messale)

ORCHESTRA STELLA D'ITALIA:—Debutto 10 Nov., 1929

TELEGRAMMI
S. SANTITA' PIO XI, CITTA' VATICANA.
Colonia Italiana di Winnipeg commemorando Patto Lateranense, presente amatissimo Arcivescovo, rinnova sensi filiale divozione e implora Benedizione Apostolica.
M. Ciufoletti, parroco.
S. M. VITTORIO EMANUELE III, ROMA.
Colonia Italiana di Winnipeg festeggia beneaugurante genetliaco V. M. protestando amore indefettibile Patria lontana.
Cav. M. Ciufoletti, parroco.
S. A. R. PRINCIPE UMBERTO, TORINO.
Colonia Italiana di Winnipeg rende grazie a Dio scampato pericolo V. A. Reale e presenta congratulazioni felicissimo fidanzamento.
Cav. M. Ciufoletti, parroco.

Chiesa Italiana del S. Rosario
Winnipeg, Man.
DOMENICA 10 NOV., 1929
Commemorazione solenne del Patto Lateranense; del genetliaco di S. M. Vittorio Emanuele III, Re d'Italia; e dell'11mo anniversario dell'Armistizio.
Funzione di ringraziameto per lo scampato pericolo di S.A.R. il Principe Umberto di Savoia.

COMITATO
Presidenti Onorari: S. Eccellenza l'Arcivescovo di Winnipeg, S. E. Mons. Cassullo, Delegato Ap. al Canada; Sig. A. Ferrante, R. Console Generale del Canada.
Vice-presidenti Onorari: Sig. ri F. Nesti, S. Mantello, J. Fabris, T. Dercola, P. A. Molaro, A. Marzola, J. Badali, Della Penta, E. Bortolussi.
Presidente effetivo: Rev. Cav. Dott. M. Ciufoletti, parroco.
Presidente Comitato Musica: G. L. Sellan.
La Societa Maschile "Roma", la Societa femminile del S. Rosario e l'Italian Young Ladies' Club interverranno in corpo.

PROGRAM OF GALA EVENING COMMEMORATING THE SIGNING OF THE LATERAN TREATY, THE ELEVENTH ANNIVERSARY OF THE ITALIAN ARMISTICE AND TRIBUTES TO KING VITTORIO EMMANUELE AND PRINCE UMBERTO, HOLY ROSARY CHURCH, WINNIPEG 1929 (HOLY ROSARY CHURCH ARCHIVES)

That Fascism was perceived to have saved the capitalist order from falling apart in Italy was certainly one of the reasons why it met with the approval of many North American businessmen and politicians.[2] Repugnance towards Italian immigrants was also a contributing factor. It was believed that "with Mussolini and fascism there was an Italian and an Italy to obliterate the image of ragged street musicians and migrant track workers."[3]

With each passing year, the chorus of voices singing the hymns of Fascism and the personal virtues of Mussolini grew louder and louder. Ontario premier Mitchell Hepburn lauded Mussolini for his determination and purpose of mind. Maurice Duplessis, leader of the right-wing Union Nationale party in Quebec, counted himself an admirer of Mussolini and believed that Quebec should emulate the pro-business Fascist economic policies. Abbé Lionel Groulx, the apostle of Québécois nationalism and a significant figure in the Catholic intellectual world, paid glowing tribute to the strong relationship between the Italian Fascist state and the Roman Catholic Church.

Praise and admiration for Fascism turned sour in 1935 when Italy invaded Ethiopia. In Canada, the invasion unleashed a wave of hostility toward Italians. The patronizing attitudes of the establishment, never so evident as in their praise of Mussolini, easily turned into suspicion. The about-face of Canadian public opinion created a sense of confusion and apprehension among Italians. They were torn between, on the one hand, their emotional attachments to family, relatives, and friends left behind in the *paese*, and on the other hand, their earnest desire to be recognized as worthy participants in the life of the Canadian nation.

The strain imposed by the outbreak of World War II may have been too much for many to bear. On June 10, 1940, Italy declared war on Canada. From coast to coast, Italian organizations swore allegiance to Canada and the British Empire. In Winnipeg, the Roma Society and the Young People's Club of the Holy Rosary Church pledged their unswerving loyalty to Canada. Father Alfonso Borelli, pastor of the Holy Rosary Church, and Pietro Colbertaldo, the consular agent, expended their energies in assuring Winnipeggers that the "Italian colony" was faithfully abiding by the precepts of Canadian democracy.

WINNIPEG, MONDAY JUNE 10, 1940 PAGE 11 No. 139

Winnipeg Italians Shocked; "It's Abominable, Crazy"

PIETRO COLBERTALDO,
ITALIAN VICE-CONSUL

FATHER ALFONSO BORELLI,
PASTOR HOLY ROSARY CHURCH

LEADERS of the Italian-Canadian colony in Winnipeg, tears in their eyes as they were interviewed a few moments after news of Italy's declaration of war reached the city, today declared Italy's entrance into the war was "an abominable thing" and described Mussolini's action as "crazy."

Unable to make any official statement because he had received no instructions, Pietro Colbertaldo, Italian vice-consul, said "I believe the Italians here will be loyal to Canada. A great many of them are naturalized Canadians. They are loyal to their country. This is only my personal opinion. I cannot say anything official."

Here 10 years

Mr. Colbertaldo was interviewed at the consular office, 266 Home St., a few moments after he had heard the radio announcement of Italy's declaration of war. He was scarcely able to speak when he first came to the door. Tears welled in his eyes as he found his voice.

"I have so many friends here," he said. "I have been here 10 years-three years and 10 days in Winnipeg."

"How will your people here feel about it?" he was asked.

"They will not be happy. They will not like it," he replied.

Abominable

Almost speechless with shock, Rev. Fr. A. Borelli, pastor Holy Rosary (Italian) Catholic church, Sherbrook St., very nearly broke down as he talked of the declaration of war.

"They don't know that they are doing to us over here," he said. "There are 10 million Italians in North America and 100,000 in Canada. This is an abominable thing."

All his own parishioners would remain loyal to Canada, Father Borelli said. Most of them are naturalized Canadians. More that 20 young men of his parish are serving in Canada's armed forces. Several are in the Canadian navy.

So Unhappy

"What will happen if they have to go to Italy and fight against their own brothers and cousins?" he asked, his eyes filled with tears. "I didn't think he would do it," he said at first, speaking of Mussolini. "This is terrible, terrible. I just can't imagine it." Then: "I suppose God will take care of everything," his voice torn with grief.

(*Winnipeg Tribune*, 10 June 1940)

The same day that Italy declared war on Canada, Prime Minister Mackenzie King ordered the internment of hundreds of Italian Canadians who were identified by the Royal Canadian Mounted Police as enemy aliens. The order was applied to Italians who became British subjects after September 1, 1922. Along with the setting up of a judicial mechanism to administer internment proceedings, the government also passed an order-in-council which called for the registration of all persons of Italian birth. Furthermore, the Office of the Custodian of Alien Property was authorized to confiscate the properties of enemy aliens.

The chain of events that followed King's announcement constitute one of the most dramatic, and perhaps saddest, chapters in the annals of Italian-Canadian history. Swiftly the Royal Canadian Mounted Police cast their net over a bewildered populace. A student of the internment saga noted that "it was not uncommon to witness women and children crying and screaming at the sight of their husbands or fathers being handcuffed and led away by the police."[4]

It was alleged that the names of many of those rounded up were indiscriminately culled from the guest book of Toronto's Casa d'Italia (Italian Cultural Centre). Were all those who registered in the guest book ardent supporters of Fascism? Did they constitute a threat to the security of the Canadian state? The answer to both is a flat, unequivocal no! Nonetheless, *raison d'état* triumphed over reason.

In cities throughout Ontario and Quebec, RCMP officers ransacked homes and businesses. In a scenario befitting George Orwell's *1984*, citizens volunteered to assist police in the roundup. Mitchell Hepburn, who once praised Mussolini, epitomized the hysteria that gripped many in Canadian society when he raised the spectre of a fifth column invasion:

> *I appeal to the able bodied men of Ontario to act for the protection of their homes and their factories, of their wives and children . . . I am not an alarmist but I am a realist. I urge the people of Ontario to become realists with me and see the dangers.*[5]

Man-on-street Grimmer as Italian News Breaks

While news boys rushed about shouting "Extra Extra!" Winnipeg's man-on-the-street paused during the noon lunch-hour today to scan the big red headlines announcing Italy's long-expected advent into the war. The news brought grimmer determination to pitch in and see the thing through.

Winnipeg's man-on-the-street were not worried, but they were eager to get the latest news of Mussolini's speech and actions. And they were not hesitant in saying what they thought the newest crisis would bring in its wake. Several expressed the opinion that Mussolini's move would bring the United States into the war. A number of others voiced their low of opinion of Il Duce's much-vaunted forces. "Now those Italians will find out what a real war is like" was typical of remarks made by the latter group. "This will give us a chance to see what those Italian airmen can do when they're not just bombing defenseless villagers." said another.

Most of the remarks were too full-blooded for publication. "The dirty so-and-so, stabbing us in the back like that" was typical of the talk about Il Duce. "So he's finally made up his mind. Well-I hope he gets all that's coming to him." said an old man, when he read the head-lines.

Lunch-hour crowds on Portage Ave. hurried about their business, apparently little concerned over Italy's decision. The crowd in front of The Tribune's bulletin boards was no bigger than usual. Two smartly dressed young women walked by engaged in animated conversation. As they passed one of them was heard to say: "I'd like to see the British navy blow Italy off the map."

(*Winnipeg Tribune*, 10 June 1940)

To add to their burgeoning woes, Italians were penalized financially. A spontaneous general boycott of many Italian businesses took place throughout Canada, and provincial governments ordered municipalities to terminate relief payments to non-naturalized Italians.

The roundup of Italians was virtually completed by October of 1940. Most of them were sent to Camp Petawawa, situated in the Ottawa River Valley. It is difficult to establish just exactly how many Italians were interned. Estimates range between 558 and 700.[6] What is certain, however, is that no Winnipeg Italians were interned.

In Winnipeg, Italians may not have suffered the same degree of hostility as did their counterparts in Toronto and Montreal, but they were subjected to the close scrutiny of the RCMP, to whom they had to report on a monthly basis. Relief payments were suspended, and in some cases travel restrictions were imposed. Activities such as the teaching of the Italian language and meetings of the Roma Society were declared illegal. These actions added to the psychological scars inflicted by constant harassment and ridicule from neighbours and co-workers, and the fearmongering being perpetrated by some elected officials. The mayor of St. Boniface, for example, strongly "requested a battalion of between ten and fifteen thousand fully trained men to be stationed in every Canadian city to protect life and property against fifth columnists."[7]

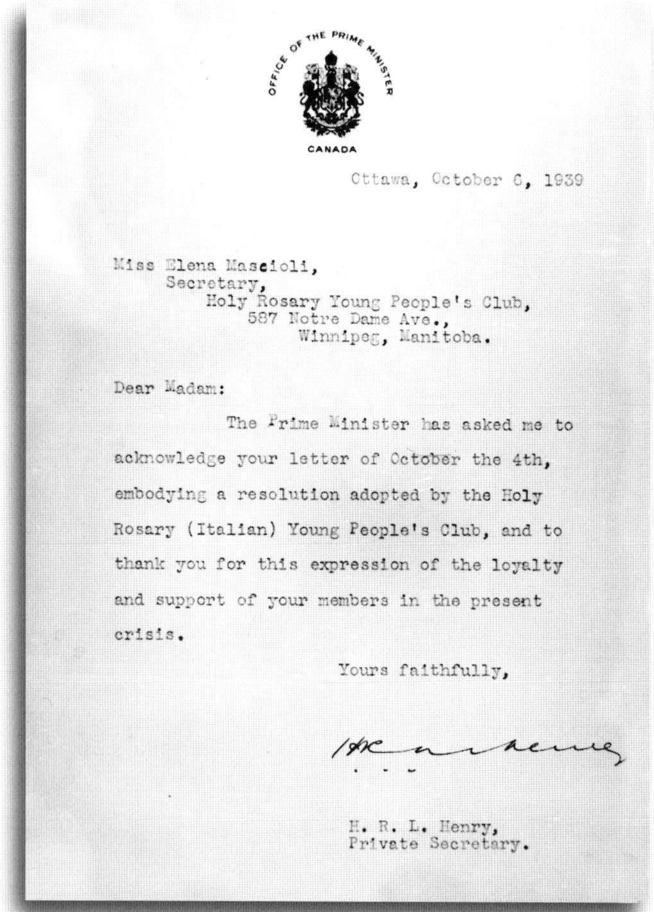
OFFICE OF THE PRIME MINISTER
CANADA

Ottawa, October 6, 1939

Miss Elena Mascioli,
Secretary,
Holy Rosary Young People's Club,
587 Notre Dame Ave.,
Winnipeg, Manitoba.

Dear Madam:

The Prime Minister has asked me to acknowledge your letter of October the 4th, embodying a resolution adopted by the Holy Rosary (Italian) Young People's Club, and to thank you for this expression of the loyalty and support of your members in the present crisis.

Yours faithfully,

H. R. L. Henry,
Private Secretary.

LETTER FROM MACKENZIE KING'S OFFICE TO ELENE MOSCIOLI, HOLY ROSARY YOUNG PEOPLE'S CLUB, OCTOBER 1939

Yet through it all, most Winnipeg Italians put on brave faces and continued their daily lives with patience and strength of character. Hundreds were to enlist in the Canadian armed forces, some in a desperate attempt to remove the stigma associated with the label "enemy alien," while others because of the inexorable conviction that the war against the twin evils of Fascism and Nazism was justified.

NOTES

1. John P. Diggins, *Mussolini and Fascism: The View from America* (Princeton: Princeton University Press, 1972), p. 18.
2. In reality, the threat from the revolutionary left had all but dissipated before the Fascists took power in 1922.
3. Diggins, *Mussolini and Fascism*, p. 56.
4. Joseph Anthony Ciccocelli, "The Innocuous Enemy Alien: Italians in Canada during World War II" M.A. thesis, University of Western Ontario, p. 60.
5. Ibid., p. 40.
6. See ibid. p. 83, *Royal Canadian Mounted Police*, report ending 31 March 1941 and Proceedings of the National Congress of Italian Canadians Biennial Conference, held 2–4 November, 1990 in Toronto.
7. Ciccocelli, "The Innocuous Enemy Alien," p. 40.

GIUSEPPE TORCHIA

In the 1930s, our neighbourhood consisted largely of French, Ukrainians, and Poles. Also there were a lot of Anglos, some of whom looked down on us because we were from another country. They referred to us as "foreigners" (in a pejorative sense), "Mussolinis," or "spaghetti eaters," which was too bad for them. However, among them there were also some very fine people who later became friends of the family.

We tried to do with what we had. We tried to make the best of life in Canada. On any given Sunday we would attend Mass and after visit relatives or friends. Auntie Angela (my mother's sister) and her family lived across the lane from us. We spent a lot of time there. Our families would get together and go on picnics on the outskirts of Transcona (we couldn't afford expensive vacations), and the children would, among other things, play baseball.

I attended the Transcona Public School until I reached Grade 9. I had no chance of obtaining a higher education because of the Great Depression. Our family had to go on relief when the CNR laid off 1,500 people; Father was one of them. I remember the day it happened. We were all waiting by the door for Dad to return from work. When he came in, he tossed his work gloves up in the air, which signified that he had lost his job. He was unemployed for four years.

RIGHT: BARBARA PUCCI AND SON VICTOR, WINNIPEG C. 1940 (VICTOR PUCCI)

VICTOR PUCCI's *parents were from Lapanno (Calabria) and came to Winnipeg (Victor's birthplace) at the turn of the century where they became prominent entrepreneurs. Though Canadian-born, Victor had problems enlisting in the navy as the result of his Italian heritage.*

I served in the navy as torpedoman in the North Atlantic and English Channel. I was treated very well except for one commander who tried to "get me." I tried to get into torpedo school and this commander heard my name being called out. He wouldn't let me apply to the school. One day, I went to school after hours and talked to a chief petty officer who was of Italian descent. He told me, "I'll get you here, don't worry." I went back but the other fellow still wouldn't let me apply. Once again I returned to the chief petty officer, who tried to reassure me. The next day my name was called out and the commander said, "You're not going." I returned to the chief petty officer, who told me to report to the school. He gave me a document that was signed by a certain Capt. Edwards, who was head of the Halifax harbour. At that moment I knew that I was permitted to attend torpedo school.

VIRGINA COSENTINO, NÉE SHERBO

During the Great Depression there was no work to be had. I remember Dad [Arcangelo Sherbo] had the shoemaker's shop. He managed to keep it open during those years, although in the winter shoemakers would make next to nothing because most people would wear overshoes and few needed to get their shoes fixed. Not only that, but very few people had the money to get their shoes fixed.

I remember that before Dad would go to work he would leave Mom some money on the dresser. This was for her to spend on groceries. Sometimes all there would be on the dresser for her was 25¢, and that was to feed the family. Sometimes he wouldn't be able to leave that much. I remember one day–it was so sad!–Dad had to admit that he made only 10¢ for a day's work. He had two rents to pay; house rent was $25 a month, as was the shop rent. Dad had a very nice landlord where he rented the shoemaker's shop. He was Duff Roblin's grandfather [former premier Rodmond Roblin], and he was a very kind man. He became Dad's customer. I remember he once told Dad, "Never mind the rent, Mr. Sherbo, just feed your family and the rest is secondary."

SAM LOSCHIAVO

As a boy living in Transcona during the Great Depression of the 1930s I remember a young man knocking at our back door. He asked for a dime. When Mom asked him why he wanted a dime he replied: "I want to buy some eggs and bread." We were having dinner at the time and Dad called to Mom to invite the young man in to join us. He ate like he had not eaten for days. He was very hungry. I have never forgotten that scene, and even today I get a lump in my throat when I think about it. After he had finished dinner he politely thanked Mom. She gave him the dime and packed some sandwiches for him. He headed across the street to a corner grocery store. The next day Mom asked the lady who owned the store what the young man had bought. She said that he had bought eggs and bread. Far from being a handout for beer, that dime was spent to provide that young man's meals for a few days. In those days, thousands of men like him, hoboes as they were incorrectly called, were riding freight trains between Vancouver and Halifax looking for work. When they tried to get off in different cities and towns the railway police would say, "Okay fellows, get back on; there's no work here; keep moving." These young men just drifted from one part of Canada to another looking for jobs that did not exist.

Many Italians with families were unemployed and were obliged to swallow their pride and seek municipal assistance or relief, as it was called in the dirty thirties. It was a sad time!

THE LOSCHIAVO FAMILY AND KIN, WINNIPEG, C. 1930. (SAM LOSCHIAVO)

PIETRO MARUCA

The dirty thirties hit many of us Italians. We shared food and clothing. Clothing was passed from one family to another with everyone being grateful and never refusing the offer. Many a time my father would cut people's hair and write their names in a little black book for credit. When they had the money to pay, their names would be scratched out. At the end of the Depression all the names in the black book had been scratched out.

ANNETTE STERN, NÉE MORELLO

During the war [World War II] my mother and dad didn't have to report to the Royal Canadian Mounted Police. I–at the age of 13–had to go and get fingerprinted. I spoke English beautifully. My mother and father spoke very little English, and yet I was considered the "traitor." Though we weren't living in Italy where the war was going on, we still felt close to our mother country, and close to our relatives. We were hoping that Hitler and Mussolini wouldn't win the war, but we were also hoping that our relatives weren't being hurt by the war. We wanted peace, which was the main thing.

THE VENIER FAMILY, WAWANESA, MANITOBA, 1928. VICTOR VENIER THIRD FROM LEFT. (VICTOR VENIER)

VICTOR VENIER's *father came to Canada from the province of Udine (Friuli) at the turn of the century, lived in Winnipeg for a few years and eventually settled with his wife and children in Wawanesa where he established a successful hotel. Although he had been born in Winnipeg, Victor experienced difficulties procuring employment with the Department of National Defence.*

During World War II my father had no problems with the Defence Department, although I did. I wanted to write government exams and some officials told me I couldn't because I was of Italian descent. I was so damn angry, because being Canadian-born I shouldn't have been treated in that manner. I did realize, however, that the position that I had applied for–radio monitoring–was a delicate position. Fortunately I had a friend in Wawanesa, Manitoba, who wrote the government a letter on my behalf and two months later I was allowed to write the exams.

I served in what was called a radio monitoring station. I was based in Winnipeg where I helped track German submarines in the Atlantic. After Germany's capitulation, I was transferred to Vancouver to monitor Japanese ships.

ITALIAN EMIGRANTS ARRIVING IN WINNIPEG, 1949. (GUERINO MACARIO)

CHAPTER 4
Emigration After 1945

In 1945, Italy emerged from 20 years of Fascism and the ravages of war barely intact. Social and economic reconstruction was a painful process as the country tried to leave its past behind and forge a new direction. This would tax the energies of all Italians but especially the working class and peasantry.

After the war, the Italian economy was in tatters. Its industrial base had been destroyed and its unemployment levels were among the highest in Europe. In the south, the peasantry clamoured for the breakup of the landed estates. Through initiatives such as the Opera Sila in Calabria, the government tried to address the inequities of ownership, but the parcels of land allotted were often too small and uncultivable. Social welfare policies and employment strategies were implemented by the Italian government but they were only partially successful in addressing the problems of poverty and surplus population.

GRIMALDESI IMMIGRANTS IN WINNIPEG, 1950S. (EMILIO ANSELMO)

Once again, emigration emerged as an important force in Italian society. In the 1950s, it was directed towards France, Germany, Switzerland and overseas countries like the United States and Canada. In contrast to the Fascist era, the post-war Italian government did everything to facilitate this process. After the war, Canada also loosened its restrictions on immigration by eliminating the "enemy alien" designation in 1947 and by opening an embassy in

IMMIGRANTS AT ESL (ENGLISH AS SECOND LANGUAGE) CLASS IN WINNIPEG, 1949. (MARILOUISE LISI)

Rome in 1948. An important aspect of Canadian immigration policy towards Italy at the time was the view that emigration was a political safety valve. A confidential dispatch sent to Ottawa from the embassy in Rome in 1948 said:

> *Surplus population is the fundamental Italian economic and social problem . . . Overpopulation means extreme poverty for a great many Italian people, with a consequent large recruiting ground for the Communist Party. The unemployed in November, 1948 numbered almost two million . . . Any increase in emigration to Canada would be of practical help to Italy in tackling her gravest problem. It would also be a small but distinctly Canadian contribution to strengthening the present democratic 'Western' government and in making less likely its replacement by Communists or by extremists of the right.*[1]

As part of this new wave of emigration, Winnipeg's Italian population increased significantly in the 1950s and '60s. In 1951 there were 1,743 people of Italian origin living in Winnipeg; by 1961 that figure had more than tripled to 4,216 and in 1971 it grew to 6,770.

Following World War II, the towns of Termini Imerese and Civita di Boiano played less significant roles in the peopling of Winnipeg, whereas Amato and Grimaldi, and the province of Udine supplied a steady stream of sojourners and settlers. Soon other towns and

CATERINA BUETI, GIUSEPPINA BUETI (NÉE BOVA), AND VINCE BUETI IN NAPLES BEFORE LEAVING FOR CANADA, 1956. (CATERINA BUETI-SOTIRIADIS)

villages began to target Winnipeg as a point of destination: San Mango d'Aquino (Calabria), Villalago (Abruzzi), Palo del Colle and Triggiano (Puglia),and Muro Lucano (Basilicata).

Between 1946 and 1961 southern Italians made up 60 percent of the 250,000 Italians who entered Canada, and 20 percent of those were from the regions of Calabria and Abruzzi. Most of these people did not constitute the "dregs" of Italian society, but actually had been able to accumulate small savings from selling their plots of land or surplus crops. Some of these emigrants were also skilled workers or artisans who were able to ply their trades in the burgeoning post-war Canadian economy. The wave of Italian immigrants consisted of carpenters, bricklayers, mechanics, tailors, and some university students and scholars as well as unskilled labourers. Post-war Italian immigrants had a higher standard of education than that of their pre-war counterparts, though their levels were still quite low by Canadian standards.

VISIT OF THE ITALIAN CONSUL-GENERAL, IN FRONT OF HOLY ROSARY CHURCH, 1955. (HOLY ROSARY CHURCH)

Throughout the 1950s and '60s Canada's immigration policy went through several changes. In the early 1950s the policy was still based largely on sponsorship and need for unskilled labour. The first wave of immigrants was largely single men recruited by the railways who would in turn sponsor their family members and loved ones. Often women would come as brides or as "picture brides." The immigration policy of 1962 which reflected the country's increased urbanization and industrialization placed emphasis on the immigrant's education, job training, and work skills. Preferences once based on ethnic background were replaced by occupational criteria.

The last major influx of Italians in Winnipeg, which occurred in 1967 and 1968, was stimulated by a joint initiative of business and government. The Canadian government played a crucial role in this process. During the months of July and August of 1967 alone, a total of 232 arrived, mostly from towns and villages near the city of Bari (Puglia). The total was comprised of 42 couples with 21 children, 94 single women, and 33 single men. The women were sponsored by the federal and Manitoba governments, and the Western Garment Manufacturers' Association of Western Canada, which had sent a representative to interview prospective garment workers in Italy.

From the early 1970s on, fewer Italians chose Winnipeg as their place of destination. Improved economic conditions in Italy made emigration less desirable, and whatever emigration did take place was readily absorbed by other countries of the European Common Market, especially Germany and France.

NOTES

1. Canadian Embassy (Rome) to Department of External Affairs (Ottawa), 8 March 1949.

L I F E S T O R I E S

The **CURATOLO** *family came to Winnipeg in the middle of the winter of 1955. Their story is told by daughter Teresa Campanelli.*

The passports were issued on November 24, 1954, and the trip on the Italian liner *Saturnia* was booked. On a cold, January morning, at the port of Naples, my parents Filomena and Umberto Curatolo bid their families farewell. On the ship, motion sickness was a problem for Filomena. She ate the cheese her mother had packed and drank only water, as she lay in the cabin. Umberto walked on deck each day and conversed with those on the same quest to lead a new life in a new land. Many of the travellers were going to Montreal, with very few continuing to Winnipeg. Filomena and Umberto arrived at the Halifax harbour on the last day of January in 1955, and boarded a train for Winnipeg.

Winnipeg was a strange, cold, and spacious city. They found themselves driving along Higgins and up Main Street, seeing the luxurious Royal Alexandra Hotel. As they rode north on Main, they saw many buildings with signs on them, signs they could not read.

They would stay at Filomena's brother's house on Inkster Boulevard until they found a place of their own.

As newcomers, they missed the life of the *paese*. Here in Winnipeg, to visit a friend, one had to make an appointment. There was no spontaneity; everyone lived so far away.

UMBERTO AND FILOMENA CURATOLO (NÉE DISTASIO) WITH DAUGHTER TERESA, WINNIPEG, 1955. (TERESA CAMPANELLI NÉE CURATOLO)

For **ANTONIO PALETTA**, *the experiences of post-war Italy and the hardship of emigration heightened his sense of social justice.*

I did not emigrate voluntarily. Most Italians of my generation did not emigrate voluntarily. Circumstances dictated that we do so. We had just gone through a destructive war which was forced on us by Fascism. The nation was poor and the resources were limited. The DeGasperi government told us that the only thing to do was to get our suitcases and leave. War veterans, peasants and workers, wretched and poor people–the lot–had to emigrate by sheer necessity and with empty suitcases.

It was difficult to leave my family behind, but because of the harsh economic conditions I had no choice. When I arrived in Winnipeg, in 1954, I started working with the CPR "gangs." I was fortunate to have found work. They were paying me 75¢ an hour, which was barely enough to cover daily expenses. The first few months in Canada were very difficult. Work on the railways was quite difficult. We workers were driven by merciless foremen. We had no say in how we were to do our work; nor did we consider protesting for fear of finding ourselves unemployed. But in all truth, the foremen were just following orders; they had no choice but to be merciless toward the workers.

I was disillusioned with life in Canada, but I never returned to Italy. I decided to leave the CPR and began to operate as a fruit and vegetable

ANTONIO PALETTA, COSENZA, ITALY, 1954. (VIERA PALETTA-MILITANO)

pedlar. I was quite satisfied with this kind of work. I enjoyed a sense of independence in this line of work which the CPR could never offer. After I sponsored my family from Italy we opened up a grocery store on Notre Dame Avenue, and then moved our business to Sargent Avenue. Subsequently my sons and daughters went into the hotel business.

I have always been interested in politics. Everybody should be interested in politics; politics is critical to the development of the human being, the family, and society as a whole. I consider myself a humanitarian who strongly believes in the importance of fraternity. I believe everyone in society should have access to all that is good in life. I don't like the fact that some are wealthy and others are poor. Inequalities based on class are unjust! (translated from Italian)

GIUSEPPE FIORENTINO *first intended to emigrate to the United States, but the sponsorship of a relative brought him and his family to Canada instead. Their story is told by his daughter Connie Fiorentino-Scerbo.*

My father [Giuseppe Fiorentino] had been a prisoner of war in Romulus, New York, from 1943 to 1945. He was impressed with the orderliness and compassion of the Americans, so much so that even after returning to Italy his intentions were to take up residence in America. In 1948, he set out to find a sponsor.

THE FIORENTINO FAMILY AND KIN, WINNIPEG, 1950S
(CONNIE FIORENTINO-SCERBO)

He sent letters to the United States and Canada. The first to respond and willing to sponsor my father was Pietro Cosentino, my mother's first cousin, to whom we as a family are most thankful unto this day.

In early 1951, my father arrived in Winnipeg to people whom he had never met, but who were very helpful and welcoming. He got a job with the CPR, but that was soon to end. He developed something on his right thumb that to this day remains a mystery. I was told that the pain was so great that eventually he had to have the thumb amputated. He was without a job at a time when there was no sick leave or medicare, and yet still had to support a family in Italy. He was terribly depressed. However, a guardian angel was with him, and he was offered a job at the Misericordia Hospital. While in the hospital for his operation, he had confided to a nurse about his prisoner-of-war years, and his work in the camp laundry. Eventually he was asked to work in the laundry at the Misericordia, where he was employed until his death in 1970.

I arrived with my mother Giuseppina, and my brother Giuseppe, in Winnipeg in October of 1953. My mother often relates how upset she was as we travelled from Halifax to Winnipeg. According to her, the bread sold on the train was like cotton batting, the scenery was depressing as we travelled through the wildernesses of Quebec and Ontario, and we couldn't understand English. She felt that we were travelling to the end of the world. No one in sight for thousands of miles! To top it all off, there was no one to meet us at the CNR station on arrival; my dad had been given the wrong arrival date.

Again a guardian angel was with us. My mom kept on saying the name Pietro Cosentino to anyone she saw. She must have thought everyone in Winnipeg knew each other as the people in Amato knew each other. Someone finally connected the name to Gus Cosentino who was working in the CNR building at the time. He came and we were saved. Gus was Pietro Cosentino's son!

What do I remember of my arrival? I remember pressing my nose on the glass doors of the CNR station and seeing a mess of dirt on what I know now as Broadway. Upon reflection, they must have been repairing something. I remember squeezing into a car next to a nice woman, Jennie Cosentino, who made me feel at ease. I remember trying to fool the children on Nassau Street, pretending I could speak many languages in addition to Italian. I remember my first days in Gladstone School, when an Italian boy (who could speak English, and I couldn't) wouldn't tell the teacher that I had to go to the washroom. I also remember seeing my mother cry over the death of her mother just four months after our arrival.

Was life in Winnipeg easy for our family? Of course not! Would life have been easier in Italy? Of course not! However, the possibilities for advancing were greater in Canada. One of my cousins always says, "If we had all remained in Italy, we would all be fighting over a square metre of land. Therefore, the many that left helped improve the possibilities and lifestyles of those who remained."

Even in comparison to the difficulties of post-war Italy, **LEO COPETTI'S** *early life in Winnipeg in the 1950s was often hard.*

With the example of my two brothers, I too chose to immigrate in May 1955. From what I understood, Switzerland, Cameroon, and Canada offered possibilities of much better wages. The first to arrive was the request from Canada for skilled labourers through our local union. Within two months, I found myself at the port of Genoa together with hundreds of other young people from almost all areas of Friuli-Venezia Giulia to cross the ocean on board the ship *Roma* from the Achille Lauro line. For the travel ticket and the obligatory $125 in cash for initial personal expenses, I had to borrow money from my brother, Giuseppe, who was married and had his own home.

At the interview with the Canadian commission in Udine, Winnipeg was assigned as my city of destination, which was practically unknown to me (I had asked for Toronto). According to them, "there was a greater possibility of work for bricklayers there." We had been given a document beforehand that forewarned us of the initial hardships in dealing with a new language and culture but we were not worried. After all, it could never be worse than what we had been through during the war where, 10 years later, you could still see the destruction caused by the bombings.

Unfortunately, later on, the first sober reality of Canada would confirm the more-than-accurate warnings we had been given.

Perhaps, as fate would have it, the first problem we

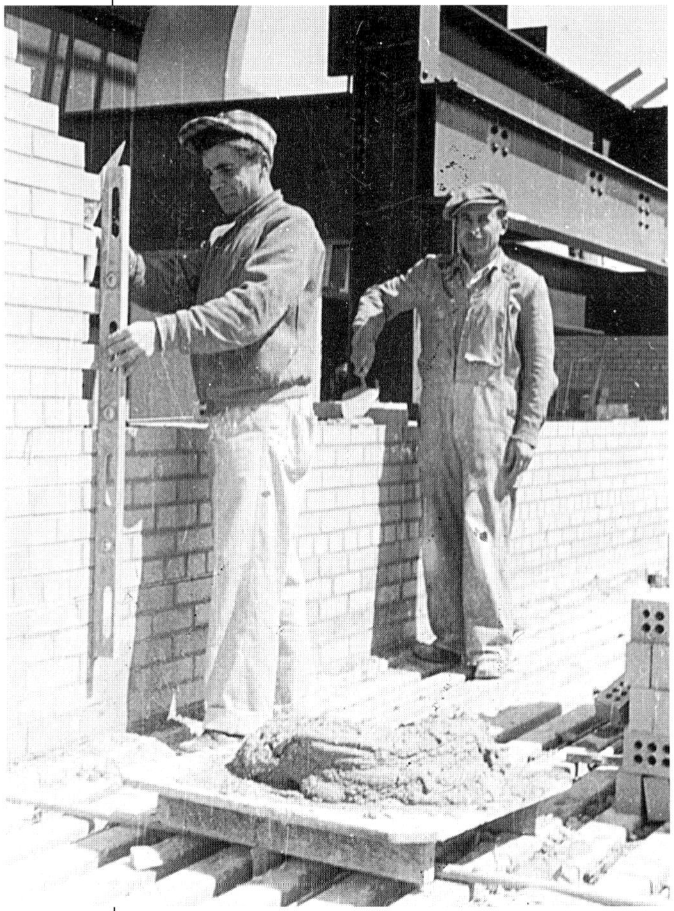

LEO COPETTI (LEFT) AT WORK IN HINTON, ALBERTA, 1956. (LEO COPETTI)

had to face was not that of Canada, but rather the ocean. After a wonderful day at sea, a day of sojourn in Barcelona, and another to cross the Azores, we travelled the rest of the nine days as ill as could be with empty dining rooms and stomachs that could not take much more. The announcement that we were nearing the port of Halifax was received with great relief and thanks to the heavens.

Before disembarking, with everyone gathered on the platform, I still remember the moving farewell from the captain of the *Roma*. At the Immigration Office in Halifax, we were assigned a landed immigrant card to be worn so that the train personnel could have us get off at the locations indicated on the cards. The trip from Halifax to Winnipeg on an old train that still had wooden benches lasted five days.

I remember that at certain railway stops, the nuns (someone told us there were even some Anglican ones, which I had never heard of before) would hand us milk and small cardboard boxes of corn flakes through the windows. Not even in the poorest houses had I ever seen someone having milk out of a cardboard box. Perhaps they thought this was a train full of prisoners of war or refugees.

The first accommodations for room and board in Winnipeg were at Immigration Hall near the CPR railway station, which the government used to sort out the continuous flow of immigrants. One of the first things I noticed here was the abundance of food even if, unfortunately, the aroma and taste of the Italian kitchen had by now vanished.

This would not be as big a problem as it was when we realized that, within a few days, we were reduced to being unable to communicate with anyone. Added to this was hearsay that, contrary to what we had been told when we left, there were not many job opportunities for us. In fact, only after many idle days did offers of work start to arrive, mostly though for labourers in the forests and on the *tracca*, Italiese, or Italian-English, for "tracks," which many, foreseeing perhaps greater difficulties while waiting, accepted without giving it a second thought.

For those who still remained unemployed, the situation started to have a negative effect on morale to the point of moving some to tears and to write home to tell the family to sell the other cow and send money for the return trip. What would be the next surprise? Would it be good or bad?

That first Sunday at Immigration Hall, a musical band wearing uniforms and playing trombones paid us a visit. "They're here to cheer us up and raise our spirits!" The day after, we learned they were from the Salvation Army.

The Polo Café, managed by an Italian family, the Fabbris, was located in front of the CPR station. It was the first place where initially we could get information on Winnipeg in a language we could understand. In fact, for many this was the first address we gave to receive mail from Italy and it was also the first after-work meeting place.

After a few weeks, we learned there was also an Italian church in Winnipeg. So one day, together with a friend made on the journey, Renato Bianchi, we set off on foot with address in hand (William and Sherbrook) asking passers-by for directions as best we could, and we managed to find it. This later became a point of reconnection, though not truly authentic, with a bit of life and culture from our native country and a place to meet other fellow countrymen. (translated from Italian)

WALTER BERTONCELLO *came to Canada in 1955 from Fellette in northern Italy. In 1960 he met and married his wife Joanne while on a brief holiday to Italy. He returned to Winnipeg, and a year later his young wife came to Canada for the first time. Their daughter Sonya Dale tells their story.*

Walter never told Joanne about the harsh Canadian winters. All he would mention to her was how beautiful springtime was, how hot the summers were,

WALTER AND GIOVANNA BERTONCELLO WITH THEIR DAUGHTERS SONYA (LEFT) AND MANUELLA (RIGHT), WINNIPEG, LATE 1960'S. (SONYA DALE NÉE BERTONCELLO)

and how colourful the leaves were in autumn. Thinking she was about to arrive in paradise, she was sadly disappointed when she reached her destination. From Halifax she made her way to Winnipeg. The beautiful hills of Quebec cheered her up, but once they were gone, the barrenness of the ensuing countryside depressed her. After what seemed an eternity, she arrived in Winnipeg. She felt terribly isolated, homesick, and, because of the language barrier, ignorant.

Eventually she made friends with the wives of other Italian immigrants, who helped her to learn English. She also found a job as a sewing-machine operator (a skill which she had acquired in Italy) in a small garment factory. She worked in the factory until her first daughter was born in August of 1962.

Prior to that birth, Joanne was to experience her first Canadian winter. This, and with the fact that she was pregnant and with no support from her family, made her feel that she was at the end of the world. Many arguments arose between husband and wife on the decision to come to Canada, but Walter truly believed that Canada offered a better life. In spite of some strong reservations, Joanne supported her husband.

TERESA MELILLO, *her husband* **MICHELE** *and their baby daughter came to Winnipeg in 1956 by way of Quebec City.*

MICHELE MELILLO AND TERESA MELILLO A FEW DAYS AFTER THEIR ARRIVAL IN WINNIPEG, 1956. (VINCENZA ENS NÉE MELILLO)

It was May 6, 1956 when my husband [Michele] and I arrived in Quebec. I couldn't believe we were here! It happened so fast! In September of 1955 we made an application to come to Canada. We had heard that the normal wait was four to five years. I can still see the look on my father's face when Michele told me we were going to Canada. He was furious! He said that we were two young "kids," married only one year and with no money. Well, we showed him! We sold everything we had and got enough money to be accepted, as we did not have a sponsor in Canada.

What would Canada be like, I thought as we rolled along the tracks. If it was anything like the voyage over, it was going to be great! I had been free of all responsibilities. My husband lay in bed seasick and a woman had offered to take care of my baby girl. I enjoyed roaming around the boat, and one night I cooked spaghetti for the crew. What fun it was to introduce these people to good Italian cooking!

We left the boat and took a train headed for Winnipeg. On arrival we took a taxi to Immigration Hall on Maple and Higgins. We spent three days there at a cost of $36. It was here that I was introduced to corn flakes and milk. I never ate so much corn flakes in my life. Amazing!

Michele decided it was time to look for work. The staff at Immigration Hall told him that a certain farmer was looking for a field hand, but when he heard that there was no room for a wife and child he decided to look elsewhere. As fate would have it, he eventually met up with a friend from Belgium. His friend took him to the CNR where he found work.

We moved from Immigration Hall to 86 Robinson Street. It was a room with a hot plate, table, and one bed. It was here that we met many friends, among them neighbours of my mother when she had been a young girl in Italy. They were good times–and bad. Yet, we had our friends, which reminded us of back home; and slowly we became accustomed to our new language and new world.

GIUSEPPE (JOE) *and* **GIUSEPPINA (MARIA) PELLETTIERI** *came to Canada through the sponsorship of Maria's brother, Pietro Perretta. Their story is told by Joe and Maria's daughter, Marietta Pellettieri.*

My parents came to Canada in 1956. They emigrated because of the "promise . . . the promise of prosperity."

RINA AND PIETRO PERRETTA, JOE AND MARIA PELLETTIERI. CHRISTMAS DAY, WINNIPEG, 1958 (MARIETTA PELLETTIERI)

Maria's brother, Pietro Perretta, was the seed from which sprang the promise of emigration for the Perretta and Pellettieri clans. Pietro was the first to arrive in Canada, whereupon he was able to procure employment as a railway worker. His main goal was to make as much money as possible, and therefore he worked as many hours as he possibly could. He always kept his eyes and ears open for better positions and often stretched the truth regarding his qualifications to secure better jobs. Once he gained a footing in this country, Pietro was able to sponsor Joe and Maria.

With big dreams but small pockets, Joe and Maria travelled by ship from Naples to Halifax. The boat trip from Italy to Canada is a momentous and overwhelming experience in the life of an emigrant; Joe and Maria were no exception to the rule. They remember the precise dates of departure and arrival. There were many mornings when the breakfast tables would be bare, for most of the passengers were suffering from seasickness and couldn't bear the thought of eating. Once on land, they felt like cattle being herded to an unknown destination.

My parents often recall the cold weather they confronted upon arrival. This not only forced them to re-evaluate their decision to come to Canada, but also confirmed their original idea of making as much money as possible so as to return to *la nostra Italia*, our Italy.

The **MARINEO** *family came to Winnipeg after first working in Belgium. Their story is told by Francesca Marineo.*

After the war there was no work in Calascibetta (Sicily), and my husband [Agatino] was forced to emigrate to Belgium in 1948, a short time after the birth of another daughter, Giuseppina. There he found work in a coal mine. After four years alone in Belgium, he wanted me to come also, so after the fifth year, he left the mine and started working as a bricklayer in a factory called La Buella. In 1953, along with my four children, I left the town in which I was born. Of course, I was not very happy to leave my sisters, brothers, and all my friends, but for the love of keeping the family together, I went to join my husband.

In Belgium, I started working in a sewing factory. They liked me and I advanced in my job. I would start at six o'clock in the morning and finish at two o'clock in the afternoon. After a year, they asked me to work in the store where they sold coats and dresses. I would work until 10 in the evening.

My husband was the type of man who wanted the best for his family, so when applications were being accepted for Canada, he applied. Our son left for Winnipeg in 1957 with two friends and went to live with my niece, Santina Lao. In 1958, after one year, the whole family emigrated. Having lived in Canada, no one liked it. The language didn't help! I immediately started working. My husband found employment after two months. We all thought of returning to Belgium.

AGATINO AND FRANCESCA MARINEO AND FAMILY, ON THEIR FIFTIETH WEDDING ANNIVERSARY, WINNIPEG, 1986. (JOSIE AUDINO)

Like many Italian families of an earlier generation, the family of **EUGENIO** *and* **CESTINA DE LUCA** *first emigrated to South America before finally arriving in Winnipeg. Their story is told by their granddaughter Adriana De Luca.*

In May 1950, the family arrived in a small town in Brazil called Barretos. They were taken to a farm owned by nonno's [grandfather's] brother, who had moved to Brazil some time earlier. The family was left to fend for itself. Not speaking the language and not knowing what fruits and berries could be eaten, they spent the first few months alone and hungry. However, after many hardships, things improved and life in Barretos soon became a time of happiness and prosperity for the family. My father and uncle no longer had to work to support the family and so were free to be kids and get into mischief, which they did often.

My nanna [grandmother] went to school to become a seamstress. She became a wonderful seamstress whose talents were sought by those who wanted the best. She eventually opened a school of her own, teaching approximately 16 girls at a time from her home.

At first my nonno was a cowboy, moving cattle through the jungle on horseback; some trips covered hundreds of miles and lasted for a month. He then became a stonemason. Eventually he would design and build buildings, Barretos' water-filter system, and even a bridge which people said was impossible to build. That bridge stands to this day. There is a plaque at the foot of the bridge on which is inscribed my nonno's name.

After learning about their successes in Brazil, I often wondered why they left for Canada. What more could they want? In a word–education. My nonno believed that Brazil could not provide his sons with a full education and future stability. The family took a vote to decide whether they would stay. The vote was three to one to leave. They never asked each other who had voted to stay.

In January 1958, they arrived in Winnipeg. Having been advised of the cold weather, they were bundled up with coats and sweaters. Yet they were still ill-prepared for the Winnipeg winter. The first few years in Winnipeg were difficult. None of them spoke English, and they only knew my nanna's sister, brother, and his wife. Moreover, they could not find jobs.

Eventually things improved. My dad and uncle took whatever jobs they could find. Nonno and nanna found jobs in the same garment factory, nonno pressing clothes, and nanna sewing. They worked in that factory until they retired. Every week nonno walked to the bank to deposit his and nonna's hard-earned money. They saved all they could and spent no more than they had to.

MICHELE RUTIGLIANO *and his wife* **GRAZIA** *came to Winnipeg in 1967.*

As a young couple we struggled and lived in a small apartment. Life did not change in comparison to living with our parents. Work became ever more important, especially given the economic conditions of Bitetto (Puglia).

Finally we heard that the Canadian government was looking for specialized machine operators and tailors to work in Canada. All expenses were to be paid for by the government. This included the cost of the flight, transportation to lodging, and initial cost of boarding until a job was procured. The news brought promises of a better life, a chance at greater opportunities and an adventure away from our small town. We wasted no time. We went to Bari within a few days of receiving the news and applied. In the morning we were submitted to a test to measure our qualifications. To our amazement we were accepted on the same day! I cannot put into the proper words the excitement that we felt. A new door had opened for us, one that would lead to a bright future in Canada.

THE RUTIGLIANO FAMILY, WINNIPEG, 1980S. (MICHELE RUTIGLIANO)

On July 12, 1967–at daybreak–we left our home town of Bitetto by car heading for Rome. Our parents drove us to Rome with their wishes of *buona fortuna.* We had an unforgettable last picnic outside of the Rome airport, which consisted of Mamma Anna's

(Grazia's mother's) *coniglio e patate al forno* [rabbit and roasted potatoes], homemade bread, and, last but not least, Papa Giacomo's (Grazia's father's) homemade wine, with which he saluted with a *brindisi* [a toast].

We left Rome by plane with a group of approximately 60 people from Puglia all destined for Winnipeg. The trip seemed never-ending, but finally at nine thirty p.m. that same day we arrived in Winnipeg and were greeted by a welcoming party of Italians. We were transported as a group by bus to the Empire Hotel (no longer standing, but located at the current site of the CNR station on Main Street). At the hotel we were provided with a room and were instructed to meet at eight a.m. the next day for breakfast.

We were left to begin our adventure that evening. Our first impressions occurred in the hotel lounge. We decided to have coffee before retiring to our rooms. We asked the waiter for *un caffé*. The waiter brought us what appeared to be a small bowl of soup. We accepted it gratefully but were unsure of what was in this concoction. After a visual investigation we decided to set it aside without tasting it and waited for our coffee. After about 10 minutes we finally asked an interpreter how long it takes for a cup of coffee in Canada. The interpreter seemed puzzled and said, "What do you mean? It's been sitting in front of you for the last 20 minutes!" To our surprise (and disappointment) espresso was not available. Without a word, we looked at each other, left the cup of so-called coffee on the table, and retired to our rooms.

EMILIO NUCCI, WINNIPEG, LATE 1950'S. (PAOLO NUCCI)

EMILIO NUCCI *was among the first new Italian immigrants to come to Winnipeg after World War II. His son Paolo Nucci tells his story.*

In the summer of 1949, my father received word that his application for immigration had been accepted. In November of 1949, he left Italy for France, where he boarded the *Santa Maria*, which would take him to Canada. The first two weeks on board the ship were quite exciting. There were a lot of activities in which he could partake. But unfortunately, the inexperience of being at sea was to rear its ugly head. During the last week he became violently ill with motion sickness and remained confined to his quarters for the rest of the voyage. Finally, the ship docked at Halifax. He was thrilled to get off the ship, not so much because he had arrived in Canada, but because he was finally on firm ground. Shortly after his arrival, he boarded a train which would take him to his "final destination": Winnipeg.

If there was one thing that my father wasn't ready for, it was the notorious Winnipeg winter. He had been warned of the extent of the severity of Winnipeg winters, but couldn't imagine the warnings to be true. Experience taught him otherwise. However, the first winter was made bearable by the new friendships he made and old ones renewed. Other Grimaldesi had been in Winnipeg, many of them having been recruited to work in the railway gangs.

Like many Italian immigrants, **GIUSEPPE CALIGIURI** *came to Canada ahead of his family. His story is told by his son Erminio Caligiuri.*

On December 13, 1956, the feast day of Santa Lucia, my father Giuseppe left Naples on the ship *Vulcania* bound for Halifax, the port of entry into Canada. On New Year's Day, he was greeted at the CNR station in Winnipeg by Zio "Mico," my father's brother. The temperature was 35 degrees below zero Fahrenheit! This was a bit of a shock for Giuseppe, who was not used to these extreme temperatures, but being a strong and healthy 30-year-old man, he took it all in stride and persevered in his faith that Canada would provide a better future for him and his family. He longed that he could be reunited with his family in the not-too-distant future.

His first job in Canada was that of a ceramic tile layer at the Winnipeg Children's Hospital, which was under construction at that time. This job lasted seven months, and in the fall of 1957, due to a slowdown in the construction industry, he found himself unemployed. After searching for work unsuccessfully for several months, he gathered his meagre belongings and on a cold Winnipeg winter day in March on the feast day of St. Joseph, he boarded a train bound west and three days later got off at Prince Rupert, a small fishing community on the west coast of British Columbia.

Within a few days, Giuseppe found a job repairing fishing boats; the work was plentiful and the money was good. He was now able to sponsor his family to Canada. In August of 1959, after over two years of separation, he was reunited with his wife and three children.

For **MATTEO MORACA** *and his family, the transition from southern Italy to the harshness of the Canadian prairies was difficult at first.*

We left my home town of San Mango (Calabria) on March 29, 1967, at five in the evening. My daughters were happy. We travelled all night in a car full of luggage and we arrived in Naples the next morning. That evening, we boarded the *Christopher Columbus*. It was about six o'clock in the evening, and like everyone, I saw all those people left on the pier. I saw the handkerchiefs waving in a final good-bye. My heart almost stopped. My thoughts returned to San Mango. The ship silently drew away from the shore, and before I knew it, all I saw was sea and sky. Before long, it grew dark and I wanted to die. I felt like I was going crazy. Staring at the sea, all you could see was dark blue. I thought I heard a voice, someone whispering to me, wanting to tell me something, but I couldn't understand.

It was a terrible voyage. My wife and daughters suffered terribly from sea-sickness. One day, we went to eat in the dining hall where we found tables already set, but as soon as we started to eat, they threw up on the table. The trip lasted six days and it was terrible.

The morning of the sixth day (April 6), we arrived in the port in Halifax, where we remained all day. At four o'clock in the afternoon, they had us board a train for Montreal prepared especially for immigrants. From Montreal we travelled to Winnipeg, where we arrived at midnight on April 8, 1967.

In Winnipeg, we found my wife's brothers and many friends and townspeople waiting for us at the CNR station. As we left the station, the streets were lit as they used to do in our town during religious festivals. I thought there was a huge party going on. When we arrived home, there really was a huge party in our honour that lasted until morning. In the light of day, I came to a realization of the situation, and to tell the truth, I wanted to go back that instant. I thought I was in hell and I immediately thought of San Mango, which I left behind with the almond trees almost in bloom. Here, looking around me, I saw only pine trees and I said to myself, "God, upon my life, this is the end." (translated from Italian)

THE MORACA FAMILY (MATTEO LEFT) ON THE SHIP CRISTOFORO COLOMBO TO CANADA, 1967. (MATTEO MORACA)

Before coming to Winnipeg, the **ESPOSITO** *family lived in northern Quebec and northern Manitoba. Their story is told by Gildetta Esposito.*

My husband Bruno Esposito, my children, Christina, Fabio, and I arrived in Canada in 1966. We left Genoa on May 7, 1966 on the *Leonardo da Vinci* and arrived in Halifax on May 14. With us there was our dog, Chaka, a German shepherd, which had become part of our family in South Africa.

This was the second time that I would leave Italy to follow my husband, a geologist. The first time was in December of 1962 when I left by boat then to go to South Africa.

The voyage to Canada was much different than the voyage to Africa. This time, the boat was full of Italian immigrants. There were many women with children who were going to Toronto and Montreal to join their husbands after years of separation. The atmosphere on board was not cheerful and happy-go-lucky. In the evening, we couldn't see the lights off the coast to reassure us of the presence of land close by. We travelled amid turbulent waters and the passengers were serious, pensive, and suffering from seasickness.

When we arrived in Halifax, I was very surprised to see the docks and all the buildings were made of wood. Our dog and faithful companion was immediately separated from us and taken to Laval, Quebec, for three months of quarantine.

Our destination in Canada was a mining village in northern Quebec called Chapais where my husband

THE ESPOSITO FAMILY ON THE SHIP LEONARDO DA VINCI TO CANADA, 1966. L TO R GILDETTA, CRISTINA, BRUNO AND FABIO. (GILDETTA ESPOSITO)

would be working as an exploratory geologist. After an endless journey by train and then by bus, we arrived at our destination only to discover that the village was completely isolated and surrounded by forests.

In 1970, we left Chapais to begin another long journey on solitary, icy roads to reach The Pas in northern Manitoba. The Pas was a fair improvement as a place to live compared to Chapais. We made ourselves a home and greatly enjoyed the weekends at nearby Clearwater Lake. At The Pas, I met my first Italian friend in Canada and began to attend classes at Internorth University.

In 1974, we finally moved to Winnipeg where we were truly happy to find an Italian community. This meant Italian language classes for our children and a variety of Italian foods on the table. We also found a house on the elevated banks of a small stream. This location reminded me of my house in Italy and made me feel more at home in Canada. (translated from Italian)

GIUSEPPE *and* **GRAZIA COLOSIMO** *were at first reluctant immigrants to Canada.*

My wife had a brother in Sault Ste. Marie and a sister in Winnipeg. My wife wanted to join her family members in Canada. My sister-in-law sponsored us, but at that time, there was a three-year wait until you were called for your interview at the Canadian Embassy in Rome.

In spring of 1961, we were called for our interview, which we attended, though we had no desire to leave Italy. We hoped that they would refuse us and deem us unsuitable candidates. The main reason we went to Rome was because we did not want to disillusion my in-laws who had made many sacrifices to be able to sponsor us, but as an old proverb says, "the Devil doesn't own the sheep yet he sells the wool." They refused many people who wanted to come, but we, on the other hand, were accepted and were given a passport visa.

Our first impression of Canada was forests and more forests. My wife would say, "Look at all that wood that we had to buy in Italy and here it wastes away in the forests." After that night and the following day, we arrived in Montreal to change trains, but the station floor seemed to move up and down like the waves of the sea while on the ship. We didn't like the food on the train, and what's more, language was a problem. Our first months in Canada, I used words that were neither English nor Italian (they were a combination of Italian and English–"Italiese"). Unfortunately, I thought they were English, but no one understood me. Later, I understood that it was a dialect created by the Italians in Canada. (translated from Italian)

Although the **LOMBARDINI** *family came to Winnipeg at the end of the last wave of Italian immigrants to Canada, many of their experiences are similar to those of immigrants in earlier generations. Their story is told by Adriana Laura Lombardini.*

We (my husband Carlo, children Paolo and Silvia, and myself) arrived on a sunny day in September 1976 smiling of empty happiness with some dreams, much fear, and all the sadness imaginable for everything dear to us that we left behind. Even though we had come to "test the waters" the year before, had secure employment and a house which I had purchased personally, at the beginning, you are always a foreigner in a foreign country where they don't speak your language, they don't know your culture or your past, your qualities, your tastes, where you don't have Mom to phone when you need help or your sister in whom you can confide your problems.

In spite of everything, our first year in Canada was our easiest because we lived it through the enchanted eyes of our children. From the first squirrel in the garden to the bicycle rides and the swings in Assiniboine Park; from the first "Big Mac" in that strange children's restaurant called "McDonald's" to the first film at the drive-in; from the first ride in a canoe on a lake that seemed like the sea to the mountain of leaves collected in the garden; from the first snowfall to the first spin on ice skates. Every day we learned something, every day we discovered something new.

Even we adults learned many things–first of all, that you can't go hunting in Manitoba on a Sunday! What to do on our first Sunday in Winnipeg? The container with our furniture was emptied, the house organized, so we thought we would go hunting as we did in Italy. We went to get the licences, packed the children, picnic basket, and, as luck would have it, at the first shots, a very frightened farmer who lived nearby came running to tell us, "No, please, no hunting in Manitoba on Sunday." The poor soul, all nervous, tried to make us understand, at first with little success and then, finally, we understood–and even more frightened than he, we left our captured trophies and returned to the city downhearted and dejected, intending to better inform ourselves in the future!

Of course, our first Christmas was very difficult. We all cried on the phone while wishing everyone a Merry Christmas. And to think that only a year before, we had all celebrated together in front of the illuminated *crèche* where, fast and furious, we adults would place the gifts while we prepared the children for Midnight Mass in the cathedral. There are moments when "reasons" no longer count.

And then life takes its course and adapts, like thin fog and empty spaces. You meet other immigrants; you make new friends. You get used to this way of life which has a vaguely colonial flavour which also has some advantages with respect to the Italian way of life– the almost complete lack of bureaucracy, for example. We gather in associations having different names but which all have an essential purpose: to create roots, to keep our culture alive, to help one another. And we learn to love the land that has welcomed us. (translated from Italian)

CHARLEY VENIER AND JOSEPH VENIER (PROPRIETOR) AT THE ROMA CAFÉ, HIGGINS AVENUE, WINNIPEG, 1911 (VICTOR VENIER)

CHAPTER 5

The World of Work

Work was at the heart of what Italians–and most other immigrants-came to Canada for. Italians in Manitoba brought with them skills and resources to make their livelihoods in their new home. For many, life in Canada meant adjusting and adapting to harsh working conditions. Work constituted an important element in the development of the Italian Canadian identity. For many, the workplace became the principal arena of interaction with Canadian society; here they were to learn about the rules, values, and norms of their new land and to meet other immigrants from all over the world.

Probably the first to come to Winnipeg was Frank Mariaggi, a Corsican of Italian origin, who arrived in 1870 as part of Colonel Wolseley's Red River Expedition against Riel. In 1902, in partnership with George Skinner, he opened a restaurant in the Alexandra Block (86 Albert Street), and in 1903 converted the rest of the building into a luxury hotel. In addition to well-furnished suites, an elegant main dining room, and small private dining rooms, there was the "grotto," four small-cave like

MARIAGGI'S HOTEL, MCDERMOT AND ALBERT, WINNIPEG, C. 1903 (WESTERN CANADA PICTORIAL INDEX)

MARIAGGI HOTEL, BACHELOR'S DINNER, C. 1905 (PROVINCIAL ARCHIVES OF MANITOBA)

dining rooms fashioned in sand and mortar knotted along the walls, the columns and behind the bar. Each room had a tiny waterfall with goldfish flashing in the low light. In addition to being a fine chef and bold hotelier, Mariaggi made a tidy sum in landholdings in Winnipeg and Port Arthur. In 1908, he liquidated all of his assets and with his Canadian wife returned to Corsica where he died in 1918.

The first Sicilians to reside in Winnipeg—Leonardo Emma and Giuseppe Panaro—opened a fruit and confectionery store on Main Street in 1892. A few years later, two other Sicilians, Agostino and Giuseppe Badali (both from Termini Imerese), operated the Badali Brothers fruit and confectionery store on the corner of Portage and Smith. By 1913, the Badalis entered into partnership with Emma and Panaro, whereupon they established the Olympia Hotel, which would later be renamed the Marlborough.

Other Sicilians were asserting their considerable work skills. As early as 1907, Nunzio Battaglia owned a fruit and confectionery store on Notre Dame. Another Battaglia–Frankie–became one of Canada's most gifted prizefighters in the 1930s. The Lama family operated Aetna Café on Portage Avenue, and Salvatore Cascisa operated a restaurant on the corner of Ellice and Princess. Charles Rocco ran the Venice Café in joint ownership with the Sicilian Frank Cancilla.

By the early 1920s, Sicilians were vying with Jews for control of Winnipeg's fruit and wholesale sectors. Throughout North America, Sicilian fruit vendors resumed the occupations they were practising in Italy. The Termitani were present in cities such as New Orleans

FRANK ALBI SR., C.1914. IN THE 1920'S, ALBI MANAGED THE MERCHANTS HOTEL IN PORTAGE LA PRAIRIE. (FRANK ALBI SR.)

as early as the 1860s, and from there developed networks throughout the United States and Canada. The Winnipeg Termitani were a dynamic group; they established a petty bourgeois foundation, which was to have significant implications for the development of Winnipeg Italian settlement patterns and social relations.

Unlike the Termitani, the people of Amato who came to Winnipeg were essentially working-class in composition. There were of course exceptions. Men like Arcangelo Sherbo, Gaetano Loschiavo, Alfonso Pingitore, and Giuseppe Fiorentino had their own shoe repair shops. The Romeo brothers–Francesco and Saverio–owned a fruit and confectionery store on Selkirk Avenue. By the late 1920s, two Amatese settlements had emerged in Winnipeg: one was in Transcona, the other in Fort Rouge. Both of these settlements were clustered

NICKY DELLAPENTA AND HIS HORSE "BABE", WINNIPEG, 1923. (HENRY DELLAPENTA)

THE VILLARBOITO BROTHERS, FURNITURE MAKERS AND WOOD CARVERS, WINNIPEG, 1930S. (MANITOBA MUSEUM OF MAN AND NATURE)

WELCH COMPANY RAILWAY GANG IN B.C.

ERNESTO AND BARBARA PUCCI (FOREGROUND) INSIDE THE PUCCI BROTHERS FRUIT AND CONFECTIONERY (490 NOTRE DAME), WINNIPEG, 1918. (VICTOR PUCCI)

near the shops of the Canadian National Railways, which employed many Amatese. There they carried out a variety of jobs: laying tracks, carpentering, painting, welding, just to name a few. Once they established their niche in the world of work, many were able to sponsor family and friends from the home town.

There were other groups that helped to define the Winnipeg Italian social experience. Immigrants from the province of Cosenza, especially the towns of Grimaldi and Lappano, helped build the railway lines across western Canada. The Grimaldesi railway contractors, Giovanni and Vincenzo Veltri (or Welch), played important roles in recruiting Grimaldesi and other labourers for the Canadian Pacific Railway Company throughout the 1890s and early 1900s. Vincenzo Veltri was a central figure in the early years of the Winnipeg Italian immigration experience. In 1911, he played a major role in the formation of the first Italian organization in Winnipeg, the Roma Mutual Benevolent Society.

The Veltri legacy was carried on by Giovanni's son Raffaele (Ralph Welch), who operated the R.F. Welch company out of Port Arthur, Ontario. In the early 1950s, the company was able to procure a lucrative contract from the Canadian government which resulted in the importation of hundreds of Grimaldesi and other Italian labourers. Ralph Welch required assistance in this endeavour, and for this he called on his friend and fellow Grimaldese Frank Albi, who resided in Winnipeg.

The Pucci brothers–Vittorio, Ernesto, Serafino, and Luigi–from Lappano arrived in Winnipeg in the late 1890s after working as railway navvies for the Veltris. No longer satisfied with a proletarian lifestyle,

ORCHESTRA AT BARONI'S CAFÉ, WINNIPEG, 1925. (PROVINCIAL ARCHIVES OF MANITOBA)

FRANKIE BATTAGLIA

Frankie Battaglia was born in Winnipeg's West End in 1910, the fifth of eleven children. His parents, Sicilian immigrants Nunzio and Angela Battaglia owned a fruit and confectionary store on Notre Dame Avenue.

At the encouragement of ex-heavy weight champion Jack Dempsey, Battaglia became a professional prize fighter. By the early 1930s he was considered one of the five best middleweight fighters in the world. On March 12, 1932 Battaglia stunned the boxing world by knocking out top middleweight contender Ben Jeby in the first round. The next year he fought and lost to Jeby at Madison Square Garden for the world middleweight title. Battaglia challenged for the world title in 1936 but was knocked out by new champion Freddy Steele.

Following his retirement from the ring, Battaglia would eventually settle in California. In the mid-1950s, he and his wife returned to Winnipeg where they managed a restaurant at the corner of Pembina Highway and Stafford for several years. In 1955, Battaglia returned to California, where he lived until his death in 1971.

FRANKIE BATTAGLIA 1929 (PROVINCIAL ARCHIVES OF MANITOBA)

...ay, July 27, 1988

Frankie was this city's finest

...Martin Zeillig

...OSTERS AND NEWSPAPER articles ...oclaimed him 'The Dynamiter, The ...nnipeg Walloper' and 'The Grea...er in the Middleweight Class.' The ...ack Dempsey said: "He had the ...a lion, but was a cool, deliberate ...at glowering dean of boxing lore, ...er, predicted that "the Winnipeg ...s as a sure champion." Chica... Harry MacNamara christened ...k prince of the middleweights." ... battles were fought in New ...endary Madison Square Gar... the cavernous confines of ...n. There were also some ...fests in the (even then) ... Amphitheatre as well as ...lympic Rink located on ... the politically hot and ... North End. It was the ... when five cents plunked ...old counter of Jack's Cafe ... steaming mug of fresh java, ...employment lines seemed endless, and when, according to sports historian Vince Leah, "Winnipeg was a great fight town."

His career knockout record was impressive — over 50 per cent, and some of his victims boasted a high rating (few of them glass jawed "bum-of-the-month palookas): Ben Jeby, KO first round; Sammy (Kid) Slaughter, KO seventh round; Joe Sharkey, KO seventh round; Paul Pirrone, KO first round, and numerous others during a 100-fight amateur and professional career. Yet the ultimate goal — the world middleweight championship — eluded him, though he valiantly challenged for it twice.

Frankie Battaglia was, in the eyes of many, the most accomplished natural fighter ever to emerge from Winnipeg. This year marks the 50th anniversary of Battaglia's retirement from professional boxing. It is also the 17th year since his untimely death from a heart attack in 1971. (Battaglia was inducted into the Manitoba Sports Hall of Fame in 1981).

The story begins Sept. 10, 1910. A son (the fifth of 11 children) is born to Nunzio and Angela, hard-working Italian emigres scratching out a modest existence in their small grocery store on Ellice Avenue. Frankie's earliest years were spent in the West End attending John M. King School, engaging in sports and dutifully delivering groceries for his mother.

The lure of the sweet science beckoned. Battaglia was a gangly, 124-pound stripling of 16 when he first donned a pair of leather boxing mitts and ducked under the sagging ropes of the squared circle at the Adelaide Avenue One Big Union (OBU) Gymnasium. His tigerish toughness and raw talent soon caught the eye of local boxing coach Jack Cancilla. Under Cancilla's patient and skillful tutelage the youthful Battaglia sharpened his pugilistic prowess.

Close friend and amateur sparring partner Frank Cancilla (Jack Cancilla's nephew) suffered the stings of Battaglia's hooks and jabs: "He had a real killer instinct as a fighter. He was all business. His punches were like something shot out of a cannon. There was only one thing in his mind — to win by a knockout. But Frankie was a great guy out of the ring."

A chance meeting with ex-heavyweight champ Jack Dempsey had a profound effect on the impressionable teenager. Emmanuel Battaglia will never forget his older brother's encounter with the famed Manassa ...auler: "One of our neighbors was Mrs. ...acIsaac who was a close relative of Demp...y. He came up to visit her one time and ...rankie met him while delivering groceries ... the MacIsaac's."

...Several years later, during Dempsey's ...t visit to Winnipeg, a *Free Press* photog...er snapped a shot of a boyishly beaming ...glia sitting next to his idol in a suite at ...oyal Alexandra Hotel. The heading over that 1932 picture reads: 'Dempsey Tells Frankie How It Is Done.' (Emmanuel Battaglia owns a framed autographed copy of that precious photo).

In 1928, Battaglia earned a berth on the Canadian boxing team representing this country at the Amsterdam Olympics. He returned sans medal, but eager to turn professional. An early pro card at the Olympic Rink featured a main event bout between Battaglia and Myles (My) Sullivan from Minneapolis-St. Paul.

Emmanuel Battaglia has vivid recollections of that fight. "Every time Frankie got hit or when he was knocked down, I swayed in my seat," says the still trim 75-year-old former amateur bantamweight. Despite a seventh-round knockdown, Battaglia battled his way back to earn a draw with Sullivan.

Soon after the Sullivan fight, Jack Cancilla wisely sold Battaglia's contract to the prominent promoter and manager Ernie Fliegle and his partner Max Winter. The Minneapolis-based duo had a stable of other promising young boxers and could offer Battaglia the top training and competition required by a potential contender. A close relationship quickly developed between the shy, curly-haired Battaglia and the bespectacled Fliegle. It proved to be a lifelong friendship.

"Frankie Battaglia became Ernie Fliegle's eyes after Ernie developed severe sight problems," recalled Max Winter, now president emeritus of the Minnesota Vikings NFL club. "When Ernie went into Billings Memorial Hospital in Chicago for detached retina surgery, Frankie sat with him at bedside all the time. It was like a father and his son."

Winter also rates the prodigious punching Battaglia as one of the five best middleweights of his era — perhaps of all time.

Under Fliegle's agile guidance, Battaglia blossomed into a top-ranked contender. On March 12, 1932, he stunned the boxing world by knocking out fourth-ranked Ben Jeby in the first round of their main-event card at Chicago Stadium.

UNFORTUNATELY, LADY LUCK forgot to cast her smile on Battaglia during the rematch. Before a delirious crowd in Madison Square Garden on Friday, Jan. 13, 1933, the wiley Jeby avenged his earlier setback to the Canadian fighter and won the vacated world middleweight title.

The next day's bold-faced headline in the *Free Press Evening Bulletin* screamed out angrily: 'Low Blow Aided In Winnipeg Boy's Defeat.' The (contentious) blow dropped Battaglia onto the canvas in Round 2 for an eight count. It was, however, a gruesome gash under Battaglia's right eye that forced referee Jack Britton to award the hometown Jeby a TKO after 12 full blood-bespattered rounds.

The flamboyant scribe for *Ring Magazine*, Paul Gallico, wrote in mock heroic style that "Frankie was beaten, bloody but unbowed. He was not his old self when he stepped in with Ben."

The two fights against Jeby rank as the dramatic peaks in Battaglia's meteoric ascent to fistic fame. He challenged for the world middleweight crown one final time. In 1936, "the larrouping tornado from Winnipeg" was knocked out in the sixth by new champion Freddy Steele (who won the title from Jeby). Heeding the sage advice of his mentor Fleigle, Battaglia retired from ring warfare in 1938.

Battaglia eventually settled in southern California with his second wife and their three children. He had one daughter from a first marriage. Small purses and some unwise investments forced him to join the mundane eight-hour, work-a-day world of the masses. He was hired as head of security for Douglas Aircraft Company. Battaglia continued, though, to maintain a keen and active interest in boxing — refereeing numerous bouts.

Frances, his second wife, recalled during a long-distance telephone chat that "Frankie was a very, very good and refined person who liked to read to his children, and who worked far below his capacity" after he quit the fight game.

Lisa Battaglia will always retain sensitive feelings and intimate impressions about her father. The 31-year-old counsellor (and graduate student) at Santa Monica College recalled him as a "handsome man with no scars on his hands or his face."

"Dad was not a disciplinarian. My father was not afraid to show his emotions. I remember him crying after he received news of his mother's death. I always had a sense of him being with me through the cigar smoke that used to linger in my hair."

Former U.S. president Franklin Delano Roosevelt once told heavyweight champion Joe Louis that he was a credit to his race — the human race."

Those same words ring true for Frankie Battaglia.

A young and adoring Frankie Battaglia gets some tips from no less than Jack Dempsey.

The Battaglia family portrait. Frank is fourth from left, back row.

Battaglia in his prime, 1933 photo.

ITALIAN IMMIGRANT WORKERS HAVING THEIR PROBLEMS

Winnipeg's Italian immigrants, brought here under the auspices of the provincial industry and commerce department are facing two major problems: a lack of finances and accomodations.

Toni Barone, language instructor for the group of about 250, has received many complaints from the group "but not one person has approached me wanting to go back home. They realize the potential of Canada and are willing to sacrifice a little to enjoy the benefits in years to come" he said. The Italians were recruited by the provincial government to help boost Manitoba's sagging garment industry.

Steve Putignano, official spokemans for the Italians, said the major problem facing the group is lack of finances. "We are obligated to put in a 40-hour work week at the minimum wage of $1 per hour. Our average take-home pay amounts to less than $36 per week," he said. Mr. Barone says the immigrants were given a "document" by the Embassy in Rome, before they arrived in Winnipeg. It guaranteed a minimum wage of $50 per week, he said.

Under provincial regulations, everyone becoming a trainee in the garment industry works for the minimum wage regardless of whether immigrant or native born. The training period is set at eight weeks and, in the case of the Italians, included a number of weekly English lessons, which were included in the 40-hour work period. Most of the Italians who arrived in July are occupied with piece-work projects and earn about $55 per week.

The group also has misunderstood accomodation procedure. "When we were contacted, we were told arrangements had been made for special accomodations for us and our families. Nothing has been done. Most of us were left on our own to fend for ourselves and have found lodging in private homes throughout the city," Mr. Putignano said. But, he emphasized, nobody seemed to want to go back to Italy. The immigrants seem willing to sacrifice salary for future opportunity.

(*Winnipeg Tribune*, 5 October 1967)

PHOTO: UNIVERSITY OF MANITOBA ARCHIVES

DON CARLOS BAND AT CASINO DON CARLOS, WINNIPEG 1949. CHARLIE MAZZONE IN FRONT WITH VIOLIN. (MANITOBA MUSEUM OF MAN AND NATURE)

they directed their energies towards entrepreneurship. They were to emerge as successful grocery store owners and wine merchants.

The immigrants from the region of Molise also made their presence felt. The overwhelming majority came from the province of Campobasso, and specifically the towns of Civita di Boiano and Campochiaro. Many of these people were to emerge as petty entrepreneurs, primarily in the fruit-vending business. Beginning in the early 1930s, the Scinocca family from Civita di Boiano operated the San Remo fruit store. Giovanni Mainella, a *paesano* of the Scinoccas, owned and operated the Overdale Coffee Shop in the St. James area. Anthony Carrelli, from Fossalto (near Campobasso), settled in Winnipeg in 1889. He was probably the first Italian to enter into business with a non-Italian, when in 1905 he opened up a tailor shop with a certain Mr.Yanchura. According to Henderson's Directory for the year 1919, Carrelli had gone into the restaurant business.

The Friulani were by far the largest contingent of northern Italians. They specialized in three occupations: brickmaking, bricklaying, and marble cutting. Many of them had practised their trades in other countries prior to entering Canada.[1] A case in point was Osvaldo Bidinosti. Bidinosti, who was born in 1871 in the town of San Daniele del Friuli (province of Udine), was an assertive no-nonsense individual whose early years in Friuli were spent learning the trade of *muratore* (bricklayer). As a teenager, he left Friuli and journeyed to Manchuria and Siberia, and worked on the Trans-Siberian railway. In the mid-1890s he emigrated to Argentina, where he carried out his trade. He arrived in Winnipeg in 1901 with his wife Ermelina, who shortly thereafter passed away. By 1912, Bidinosti had accumulated enough savings to purchase farmland near Petersfield, Manitoba, with fellow Friulano, Antonio Vit. Vit died in 1943, and Bidinosti in 1956.

The majority of Winnipeg Italians in the period up to the 1930s were men without women. They carried the dual responsibilities of supporting themselves and sending portions of their meagre savings back home

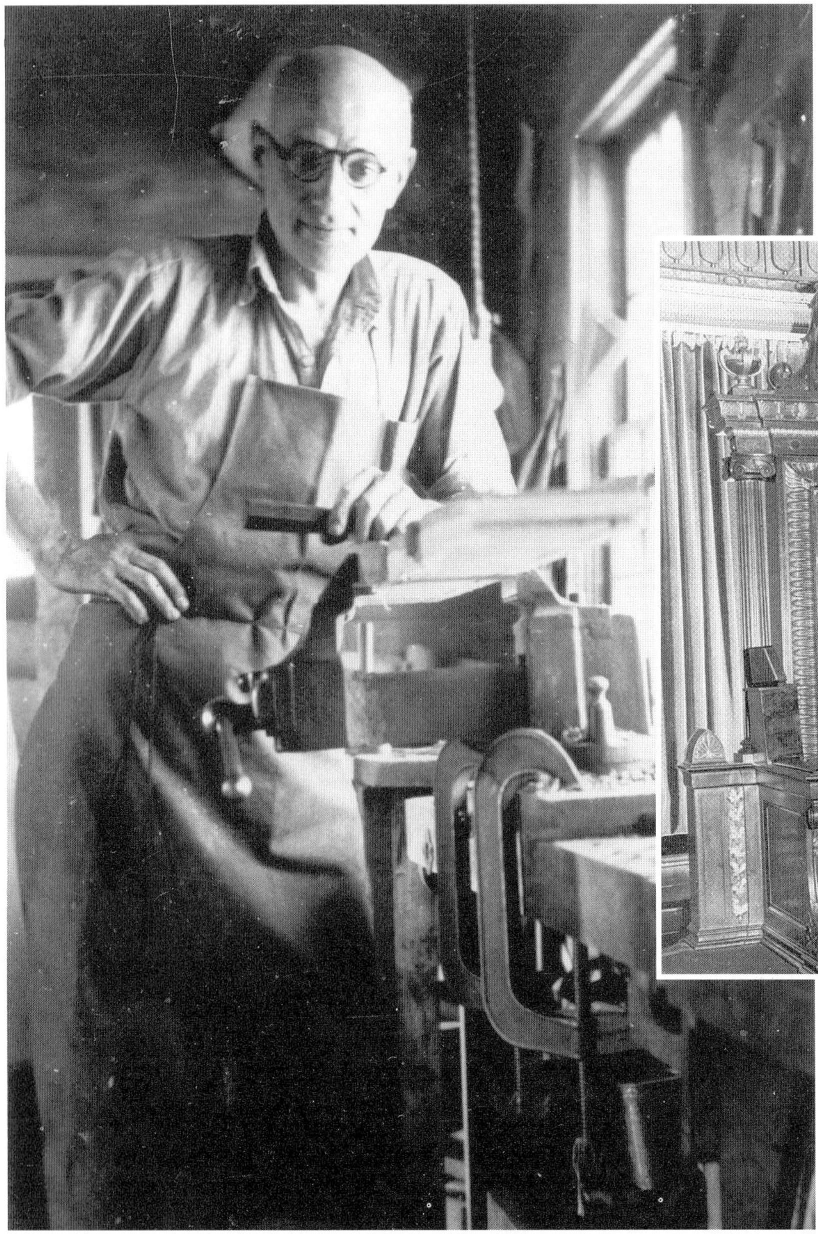

to their families in Italy. Official society, in the form of politicians, business people, social workers, religious leaders, and journalists, often castigated them in greatly exaggerated terms for their "voracious sexual appetites" and immoral conduct. The image of the "dirty navvy" (in both the physical and moral sense) became a hallmark of social Darwinism and other racial doctrines.

CARLO FUSETTI, WOOD CARVER AND FURNITURE MAKER, WINNIPEG, C. EARLY 1970S. FUSETTI CARVED THE SPEAKER'S CHAIR IN THE MANITOBA LEGISLATURE. (MUSEUM OF MAN AND NATURE)

The drama that unfolded in front of these men, who were derided by the establishment as "birds of passage," was equalled only by the experiences of the women and children they left behind. These women often had to take responsibility for heavier work. In the absence of their husbands or fathers, they also became the family decision-makers. These new roles would subtly affect their relationships with their menfolk when they were eventually reunited.[2]

The skills that they acquired to maintain the household back in the *paese* proved to be essential to the survival of the family in Canada. Italian women also played an important role in the operation of family businesses. They provided the labour power and advice needed to ensure that all aspects of the business ran smoothly. In addition to managing household duties, some women entered the labour force. Prior to World War II, those Winnipeg Italian women who worked outside the homes performed jobs that seemed extensions of their household duties. For example, Henderson's Directory for the year 1939 lists them in following occupations: store and sales clerks, packers, dressmakers, and stenographers.

This began to change after World War II. In order to augment the development of trade, service and newer industries, the Canadian government's immigration policy assisted business in the recruitment of large reserves of cheap labour. In contrast to earlier periods, female immigrants were now being encouraged to fill places in many industries. From 1945 to 1975 over three million immigrants came to Canada. Almost half of these were women. One industry in particular that benefited from this influx of immigrant female labour was the garment industry.

Like other immigrant women, Italian women played a seminal role in defining a "working-class family strategy for success." The wages made by female immigrants helped support families through periods of male seasonal unemployment. Often, women's earnings paid for daily living expenses, while men's paycheques went into savings accounts towards the purchase of a house.[3]

While that sector of the working class that goes by the description of manual and unskilled labour represented a sizable component of the Winnipeg Italian population into the 1970s, there was a noticeable increase in the number of foremen, supervisors–in short–those occupations often associated with the "labour aristocracy." There was also a steady rise in the number of college- and university-educated Winnipeg Italians. Many were to enter into a variety of professions such as business administration, law, science, medicine, teaching, and government civil service.

From the early days of the Termitani and Boianesi fruit vendors, private entrepreneurship has been a regular feature of Winnipeg Italian history. Throughout the post-war era, Italian-owned restaurants, hairdressing salons, grocery stores, masonry contracting firms, real estate agencies, and tailor shops dotted Winnipeg's economic landscape at an unprecedented level. Businesses such as Mama Trossi's Restaurant and the Rancho Don Carlos, a nightclub owned and operated by Carlo "Charlie" Mazzone, were popular with Winnipeggers of all backgrounds in the 1940s and 1950s. Many of these businesses were family ventures, a factor that may go a long way in explaining why they were able to demonstrate a remarkable degree of resiliency during periods of economic slowdown or recession, and in an age in which monopoly capitalism was casting its ominous shadow.

Notes

1. On the Friulani, please see Zucchi, *Italians in Toronto*, pp. 84–87.
2. Gladys DeSchepper, "Immigrant and Female," *Homemaker's Digest* (1976), p. 1.
3. Franca Iacovetta, "From Contadina to Worker: Southern Italian Working Women in Toronto, 1947–62", *Polyphony* 7, no. 2 (Fall/ Winter 1985) p. 94.

L I F E S T O R I E S

The **BADALI** *family was among the first Italian entrepreneurs in Winnipeg. Their story is told by Agostino Badali's granddaughter, Pat Olsen.*

Agostino Badali and his brother Giuseppe opened a fruit store on the northeast corner of Portage Avenue and Smith Street in the early 1890s. Agostino and his family lived above the store. Although being far from the centre of trade on Main Street, the shop did well as business gradually moved west. When the Kensington Building was erected on that corner, the Badalis opened the Olympia Café on the site of the former store. In 1905, Eaton's, the *Free Press* and other firms followed the trend to Portage Avenue. As a result, Olympia Café was an overwhelming success.

In 1913, the Badali brothers along with Leonardo Emma and Giuseppe Panaro acquired property further north on Smith Street and a year later opened the Olympia Hotel (later renamed the Marlborough). The Olympia Hotel was described by the *Hotel and Travel Magazine* as "the miniature hotel-de-luxe of Canada." No expense was spared as marble, stained-glass windows, brocades, and fine furniture were imported from Italy, France, and England. Unfortunately after the war came the economic boom turned into depression. The hotel closed its doors in 1915, and so ended the dream of these four men who chose the least favourable time to enter into a business partnership. By 1917, the Badalis and Giuseppe Panaro started all over again by opening the new Olympia Café on Donald Street.

In 1911, Agostino bought property on the Assiniboine River in what is now Westwood. There he built a cottage, where he and his family enjoyed vacationing for many years. Years later, his son Frank built a home on this property. Here Agostino Badali lived with Frank and his daughter Sena (whose husband had died in 1959) until his death in 1976 at the age of 94.

AUGUST BADALI (LEFT) INSIDE THE OLYMPIA CAFÉ, C.1913 (SENA BADALI)

FRANCESCO LOSCHIAVO *was one of the many Italian immigrants who worked for railway contractors in the early part of this century. The story of his working life is told by his son, Sam Loschiavo.*

Soon after arriving in Winnipeg in 1913, my father got a job with Mackenzie-Mann, a contracting company that was building railway lines, and hiring most of the immigrant workers. Men looking for work would congregate at the old Winnipeg city hall where agents of the company would hire groups of men and send them to various places in Manitoba, Saskatchewan, and Alberta to build railroads.

Dad spent several years working in these provinces. Initially, it was not his intention to remain in Canada. Like many young men of his time, he thought that he would earn enough money over a few years and then return to Italy. However, that dream was not to be fulfilled, as many, sadly, earned little. The work was only seasonal and the wages low. The men were laid off from November to May. To save money they lived together in groups in boarding houses, two to four men in a room. Board was cheap by today's standards–$3 a month and sometimes that included laundry. It was a hard life. There wasn't much socializing except among themselves, playing cards, conversing, or writing letters home. Their limited knowledge of English prevented them from becoming part of the larger community. They were considered dirty and unkempt. This was the image that the "establishment" had of all Continental Europeans, not just Italians. Very little compassion or understanding was shown to these "outsiders."

The Scerbos ran a small grocery store and boarding house for young Italian male immigrants. It was there that my father met Caterina Scerbo, whom he married in 1923. In the late 1920s my parents opened a store on Transcona's main street (Regent Avenue) and named it Tivoli Confectionery. My mother was a good manager and built up a clientele of steady, loyal customers due largely to her kind, friendly, and generous disposition. Katie, as she was fondly known, had a reputation for having the largest, most creative, and tastiest banana splits and sundaes in town. She probably made no profit on them but the pride of satisfying people and their appreciation was reward enough. Even when family, relatives, and friends praised her cooking she was modest about accepting the praise. However, I am sure that she was secretly pleased.

Her ice cream parlour was always full, and yet it was also the place where many a romance began and blossomed. Katie also sponsored a senior girls' softball team called the Tivolis, and after their games the girls would congregate at the ice cream parlour with their boyfriends. Mom had many roles–wife, mother, storekeeper, sponsor, matchmaker, and "mother confessor" to the team. When the team would win a league championship my parents provided a banquet and dance in celebration.

The business helped support the family and others through the 1930s when work at the railway shops was scarce. In 1948, my parents opened a store on Sargent Avenue. However, the coming of supermarkets sounded the death knell of small neighbourhood stores. The business was sold in 1955 and my parents went to Italy for a few years so that Dad could care for his mother whom he had seen little of since 1913. They returned to Transcona in 1964, where they spent the remainder of their lives.

CARLO (CHARLIE) MAZZONE *operated Rancho Don Carlos in the 1940s and 1950s. For many years, it was Winnipeg's premier night spot.*

I started working with the Canadian Northern Railways when I was 12 years old. I started working September 11, 1917, on a Saturday afternoon. I worked

CHARLIE MAZZONE (RIGHT) GREETING BOB HOPE AND JERRY COLONNA (BEING INTERVIEWED BY CLIFF GARDNER) ON THEIR ARRIVAL IN WINNIPEG, 1955 (WESTERN CANADA PICTORIAL INDEX)

11 hours a day and every day and got paid 17¢ an hour as a water boy. My father was a track foreman, and I used to supply water to his workers. I used to carry two buckets on my shoulders. I did that for two years. I also worked as a car helper, sandblaster, and did office work. I did all kinds of jobs in the shops.

When I worked at the shops I would study music at night. I would also visit nightclubs in the United States. I organized a band called Curley's Music Weavers and our slogan was "the boy who makes you dance." I used to play at Ukrainian picnics and Italian picnics way out in the bushes. What I call bushes is the present-day busy intersection of Stafford and Pembina. At the time, you could see deer and rabbits there. I also played in the North End. I played at the Manitoba Hall, the Travellers Hall, and the Oddfellows. I took over the River Park Dance Pavilion. It had a shooting gallery, bowling lanes and horse racing. Now there is a residential area there. It was like a recreational area. I had a dance hall there that could accommodate 1,500 people. In those days it was a dime a dance. You would buy 10 tickets, go to a girl, and ask her for a dance. You gave one ticket to the attendant and went through the gate with the girl.

I only had $4,000 when I first started bringing in bands. The first act I brought was the "Cornhuskers." They cost me $760. It was pretty tough to get the money back, because people weren't used to it, and they didn't know of the "Cornhuskers."

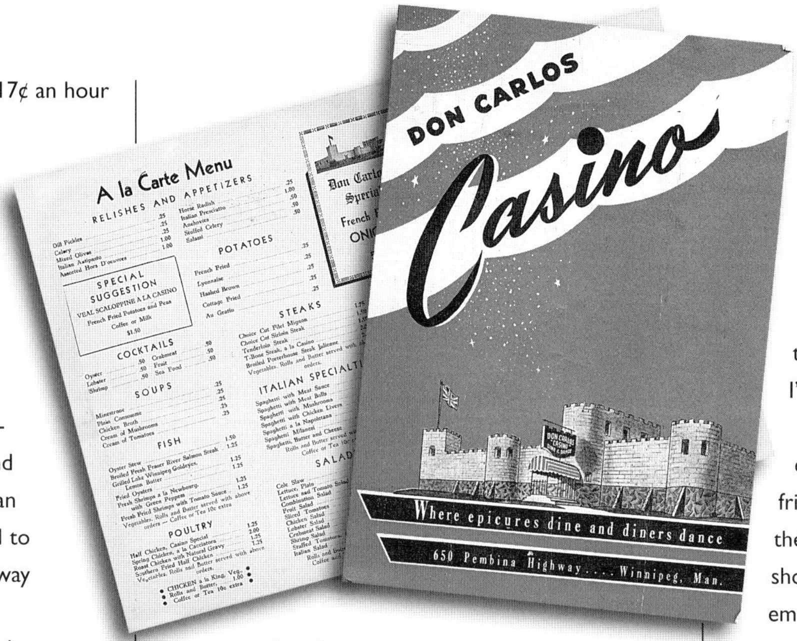

MENU COURTESY CLIFF GARDNER

The next one I brought, at the time was one of the top names–Red Norvo. I paid him $3,000. I had no luck on the opening or on the second day. I was sunk for $3,000; that would have put me out of business. So, I went to the *Free Press* where I knew a fellow there who was the city editor–Albert Booth. I said, "Albert, I have a little problem. If you could help me." He said, "Well, what do you want?" Well, I said, "Look, I'm having Red Norvo, and every night we're booked solid; people are coming by the hundreds, and I'd like to tell people not to come this week, but to try to come next week. If you could get some one to write an article about the Red Norvo show?" He said, "I'll do that." So he took me over to Frank Morrison, who was a writer who didn't care for jazz. He wrote about classical music. But he did a tremendous job. He wrote that Charlie thanks the Winnipeg public for their great response, but urged people not to rush to the show this week, but to go the following week. In addition, I put an ad in the *Free Press* and *Tribune* mentioning that we were sold out. I went to Red Norvo and told him, "If you give me the extra week at a fair price, I might have a chance to come up with the money." He said, "Charlie, I'll play the next week for nothing, as long as you get out of the hole." Every night we used to close the doors and we asked about 20 or 30 friends to stay outside the building and pretend they wanted to get in. This indicated that the show was sold out. The band would play to an empty house for about five days. The following week it played to a capacity house every night. We got our money back and Red Norvo went away happy.

The place that Red Norvo played at was the Oddfellows Hall at 293 Kennedy. Then I changed it to The Fifteen Stairs, and then Don Carlos Castle, which was a nightclub and eating place. Then I started the Don Carlos Casino in the 1940s at 650 Pembina Highway. It burnt down and was rebuilt as the Rancho Don Carlos. I brought into Winnipeg all the big names. The only person I didn't bring was Frank Sinatra. But I brought in everybody else. I brought in Bob Hope, Count Basie, Louis Armstrong, Sophie Tucker, Nat King Cole, the Four Aces, the Four Lads, the Ames Brothers, the Marx Brothers, Dick Contino, Cab Calloway, and Al Martino. Just name them and they were here!

FEDERICO PAPETTI *came to Canada in 1951 and worked in many locations before settling in Winnipeg.*

I worked as a section man in West Edison, an isolated place between Kenora and Vermilion Bay. My wife and I lived in the section house, a wood house two metres from the railway. On the other side at least four metres away, there was Lake Edison, where one could see the reflection of the birch trees. There was a beaver's nest near the spot where we would get water. The beavers never did get used to our presence. They would beat their large tails emphatically every time one of us would appear.

Three years later, I got a job with Molson's in Manitoba. There were other Italian families here, but still no electricity or water in the house. The well provided hard water that smelled of boiled eggs. Later, we went to Whitemouth where we had electricity, a school, a bank, two stores, and a hospital. In the meantime, during the period I worked for the railway, four children were born. Another two were born in Whitemouth.

In 1964, I applied to work on the cranes. They offered me a choice: either Thunder Bay (in those days it was two towns: Fort William and Port Arthur) or Transcona (Winnipeg). If it were not for the fact that Bruna's (my wife's) family lived in Winnipeg, we certainly would have chosen Thunder Bay because it seemed more like my home town of Abbazia. (translated from Italian)

FEDERICO PAPETTI AT WORK, EAGLE RIVER, ONTARIO, 1958.
(FEDERICO PAPETTI)

EMILIO *and* **TERESA NUCCI** *were among the post-World War II immigrants who became entrepreneurs. For many years, they owned and operated one of Winnipeg's best-known Italian grocery stores. Their story is told by their son Paolo Nucci.*

After their marriage, my parents rented a home on Spence Street. Soon after, they relocated to 664 Corydon Avenue. It was during their stay on Corydon that my parents had four children.

One day my father discussed with my mother the idea of setting up a business. His idea was to give Winnipeg something which it did not have: a grocery store which shelved strictly Italian products. Soon he began to make inquiries as to how this could be achieved. After many phone calls, countless letters, and good old-fashioned persistence, "Nucci's Imported Foods" became a reality.

The business started out small; my parents opened it in the basement of their home. They ordered their products from various companies in Toronto, Montreal, and Italy. At the time, my mother had quit her job to run the business. My father maintained his job so he could provide additional money to the business. My grandmother helped tremendously by caring for my eldest brother.

By 1961, the business was thriving. My father quit his job and dedicated himself completely to the business. That year he built a 500-foot extension to the home and expanded the business. This allowed him to house more inventory and order a larger variety of products. The business was really the embryo for the emergence of Little Italy on Corydon. Today Little Italy is alive with restaurants, cafés, boutiques, and grocery stores. It has become a popular spot for Winnipeggers and tourists alike.

The business closed its doors on April 15, 1994. Like the saying goes, "all good things must come to an end." But it will always bring pleasant memories to my family.

For **GIUSEPPE** *(Joe) and* **GIUSEPPINA** *(Maria)* **PELLETTIERI**, *like most immigrants, hard work and frugality were a way of life. Their story is told by their daughter Marietta Pellettieri.*

Many in the Pellettieri and Perretta families worked in hospitals or factories. The English phrase that was used most often in the early years was, "Gotta job for me?" For over 20 years, Maria worked as a sewing-machine operator (on piece work, which meant she was not paid an hourly wage but on the basis of what she produced), while Joe worked as an orderly for the Manitoba Cancer Foundation for over 35. Without any skills related to their respective jobs, but with a strong and determined disposition, they excelled in the world of work. Like most immigrants, they were committed to their family and building a foundation for their future. In order to ensure that the children were never alone, Italian couples worked opposite shifts. In this scenario, men and women contributed to child rearing.

Being accustomed to living with limited resources in Italy, my parents learned the "art of frugality." This served them well in their early years in Canada. For example, they would often walk miles to save money that would have been spent on bus fare.

When **VITTORIA** *and* **ROCCO CARBONE** *came to Winnipeg, they found it difficult to adjust to living and working conditions.*

In May of 1960, with the prospect of improving our standard of living (which in retrospect was not so bad), my husband emigrated to Canada. He had been sponsored by his brother Salvatore who had been living in Winnipeg since 1956. After five months, the rest of the family joined him.

At first, life in Canada was quite difficult. It was a new and strange environment. The winters were cold and the language difficult to speak and understand. My husband's job–presser at a garment factory–was altogether different from that which he had in Italy. In many respects it was inferior to what he was doing in Italy.

THE CARBONE FAMILY, WINNIPEG, 1962. L TO R CATERINA, ROCCO, VITTORIA AND STANISLAO. (VITTORIA CARBONE)

Almost immediately after my arrival, I started to work. For 30 years I worked in a garment factory as a sewing-machine operator. In the beginning we had no car, so I had to take the bus to work. That was quite an experience. On the bus I would be surrounded by people whom I couldn't talk to. On cold days I would have to wait for long periods of time to catch a bus; in the morning I would wait for the bus in darkness to take me to work, and in the evening after work I would be waiting for the bus in darkness.

Work was difficult; my wages were not proportional to the amount that I was producing for the company. But at the same time, through work I was able to meet other people, especially other immigrant women with whom I shared similar experiences.

Eventually, as a family we slowly adjusted to life in Canada. Our children started going to school, making it possible for them to adapt to life in Canada.

My husband and I returned to Italy for a visit in 1975. At the time my mother was still alive. Things had changed dramatically–for the better. It was like night and day. My husband and I had often considered returning to Italy permanently, but because of our children, who had become accustomed to life in Canada, we decided to stay.(translated from Italian)

The **RUTIGLIANO** *family was among the wave of post-World War II Italian immigrants who came directly to manufacturing jobs. Their story is told by Michele Rutigliano.*

The next morning [after our arrival in Winnipeg] we were gathered to meet our prospective employers. We were approached by a representative from Jacob and Crowley, a garment factory. We accepted his invitation for a tour of the factory and that afternoon were told to start working on Monday.

Although our trades were the same as those we practised in Italy, the jobs in the factory here in Winnipeg appeared different, sombre and larger than life. The factory was large; many people worked in one area without talking throughout the day, and the atmosphere was very serious and at times depressing.

Within a few days of our arrival we settled into a small apartment. The first three months in Canada were very difficult for us. Not only did we miss our families, but we could not speak the language.

During the day we worked in the factory and at night we attended an English language class. With time we understood the reasons for the atmosphere in the factory and what was being said around us; we accepted our new life as best we could.

MATTEO MORACA

After arriving in Winnipeg in 1967, our suitcases and trunks remained closed for a week. I wanted to go back [to Italy] at all costs. I did not find peace during the day or night. But how could I return with my whole family, and when I had sold everything in town! Anyway, with time, I slowly calmed down and went to work for Pioneer Electric. It wasn't a job I particularly liked because what I really wanted to do was work in construction. I tried everything to change jobs to the point where I found work with Trevi Tile. I worked there two months because not even that job was satisfying.

One day, I met fellow townsman Vincenzo Costanzo, who worked in construction. I asked him if there was work for me as well. He told me to be ready at seven o'clock the next morning and he would take me to where he worked. He came by the next morning in his car and took me to the site, where we found the foreman, Mr. Silvio Molinari (born in Aprigliano in the province of Cosenza), who gladly put me to work.

For the first couple of days, I was uncomfortable because the construction industry in Canada was very different from the one in Italy. But in that particular group, they were almost all Italians and the boss, Mr. Kurtz, was very nice. I worked near my friend Costanzo and Mr. Saverio Loria (from San Giovanni in Fiore in the province of Cosenza), a good man who later became a close friend. I slowly began to concentrate on working as a bricklayer.

After a year, I found work in the evenings as a building cleaner. I would leave at seven in the morning to go and work in construction until four o'clock and then I would take a bus to go and clean until eleven-thirty, returning home at midnight. I did this for 15 years from September 1968 until 1983. Then I could no longer do it, as I was also ill. I left the construction industry, and two years before retiring, I decided to visit Italy. (translated from Italian)

Roma Society Band, 1925 (Lucy Mottola)

CHAPTER 6

Home and Social Life

As the number of Italians in Winnipeg grew after the turn of the century, several distinct communities developed. By the late 1920s a stable Italian population began to emerge in the West End, and the areas around Young, Langside, and Sherbrook Streets, bounded by Sargent Avenue on the north and Portage Avenue on the south, became known as Little Italy. North of the Sargent Avenue boundary were the CPR Weston Shops, which employed many Italians. For the Termitani and Boianesi fruit pedlars the West End was a convenient location in which to reside because of its close proximity to Market Square, then the centre of Winnipeg's trade and commerce, where they would gather together each morning and fill their wagons with fresh produce. Until 1919, the consular agent Count Giuseppe Barattieri di San Pietro had his office in the West End. In the 1930s the new consular agent Angelo Marzola established his office in the West End. The Italian Catholic parish, Holy Rosary Church, was located on the corner of Sherbrook and Bannatyne. In short, an Italian *ambiente* (environment) emerged within the confines of the West End.

YOUNG STREET, WINNIPEG, 1992

By the 1960s the West End began to witness a steady decline in its Italian population. Several factors contributed to this process. Winnipeg's rapid suburbanization engendered a relocation of businesses and industries. Suburbs such as Fort Garry, Charleswood, North Kildonan, and West Kildonan became major population centres. The proliferation of the automobile and the expansion of road routes and transit services contributed to this growth. These areas attracted a new generation of Winnipeg Italian entrepreneurs and professionals who interpreted suburban living as a natural complement to their enhanced socio-economic status. Italians were to play an important role in the economic and cultural vitality of these emerging suburbs, as epitomized by the emergence in the 1960s of Little Italy on Corydon Avenue. Today, Corydon's distinctive Italian-Canadian culture is complemented and influenced by other ethnocultural identities, creating in the process a rich and multifaceted socio-economic texture.

In the 1920s, in addition to the West End, smaller Italian enclaves emerged in Transcona and Fort Rouge. Many of the Amatesi were pulled to these areas because of the presence of the Canadian National Railway shops. A cluster of Sicilian families resided in the St. Boniface area.

Regent Avenue, Winnipeg, 1911 (Provincial Archives of Manitoba)

These communities also grew through the "commerce of migration" and the boarding-house system. Most of the Italians who emigrated to Winnipeg prior to World War I were born and raised in a semi-feudal/pre-industrial milieu. Many could not quite adapt to the tediousness and drudgery associated with wage labour. The Italian psyche was moulded in the less chaotic world of the *paese*, and the stress and strain of regimented life were too hard for it to bear. Some were to resolve this matter in part by becoming private entrepreneurs. These vendors and others became the core of an emerging Winnipeg Italian petty bourgeoisie. They served as important intermediaries in the commerce of migration by sponsoring their *paesani* who would provide much-needed labour power for the local economy.[1]

As well as acting as sponsors, many provided room and board for their newly arrived paesani. For these new arrivals, the boarding house served as a symbol of stability. Living with a *paesano* and his family satisfied the emotional need to maintain ties with the ways and customs of the old country.

The boarding-house experience was part of the immigrant's transition from sojourner to settler. For many, this meant a transition from a world made up mainly of single men to one in which the family predominated. In Italy, the family was the central feature of Italian life. More than just a set of biological arrangements, it was the major instrument of socialization, and it defined sex roles and constituted the basic mode of economic organization. In her thesis on Italians in Calgary, Antonella Fanella rightly noted that immigration reinforced codes of privilege and obligation within the nuclear family.[2] In Canada, the family maintained its primacy and contributed enormously to the social, cultural, psychological, and moral identity of Winnipeg Italians. It also served as the main vehicle for the retention of cultural and linguistic traditions.

Boarding arrangements could be found throughout Winnipeg. The Amatese Angelo Scerbo, who came to Transcona around 1910, operated a fruit and confectionery store on Regent Avenue and converted the upstairs rooms into lodgings for Amatese men working for the Grand Trunk and Transcontinental Railways. In the early 1920s, Scerbo sold the building to a Spaniard, and thereafter it was popularly referred to as the Casa du Spagniulu (Amatese dialect for "the Spaniard's house").

Winnipeg's West End, which contained a sizable number of Termitani and Boianesi in the 1920s and '30s, abounded with boarding arrangements that linked *paesani* and recreated kinship and familial ties from the old country. Italian railway workers often boarded in homes that were conveniently in close proximity to their workplaces. In addition, boarding in a *paesano*'s home was relatively cheap in comparison to rooming in a hotel or hostel, and less impersonal. Moreover, if the working-class boarder lived with a family of business people, he might be able to learn certain tricks of the trade which could serve him well in the future.

For the small businessman, taking a boarder may have satisfied a familial obligation, but it also carried with it financial benefits. The boarder, after all, was not only paying rent, but he could also be a prospective employee in the family business; thus his labour power could be harnessed to generate profits. Love of family and profit maximization united in perfect symmetry.

The practice of boarding also enhanced the personal prestige of the proprietor. An individual or family that had taken one or a few boarders was seen as providing a humanitarian service. In turn, each boarder was potentially a disseminator of the virtues and special attributes of the host family. The family was certainly critical in forging a Winnipeg Italian social identity, before religious and secular organizations had been created to meet the variety of economic, spiritual, recreational, and intellectual needs that arose. In time, however, family, church, and secular activities became closely interrelated.

The first Winnipeg Italian mutual-aid organization was the Società Roma: Società Italiana di Mutuo Soccorso (Roma Mutual Benevolent Society). Its first executive, elected at a general session held on January 9,1911, consisted of the railway contractor Vincenzo Veltri (Welch) as president, the entrepreneurs Pasquale and Frank Cancilla as the two vice-presidents, the building contractor Ernesto Marchetti as treasurer, and the tailor Anthony Carrelli as secretary of finances. While the leadership in the first and ensuing executives was predominantly petty bourgeois in nature and exclusively male, the general membership was fairly eclectic, including a broad representation of working-class Italians of various regional backgrounds.

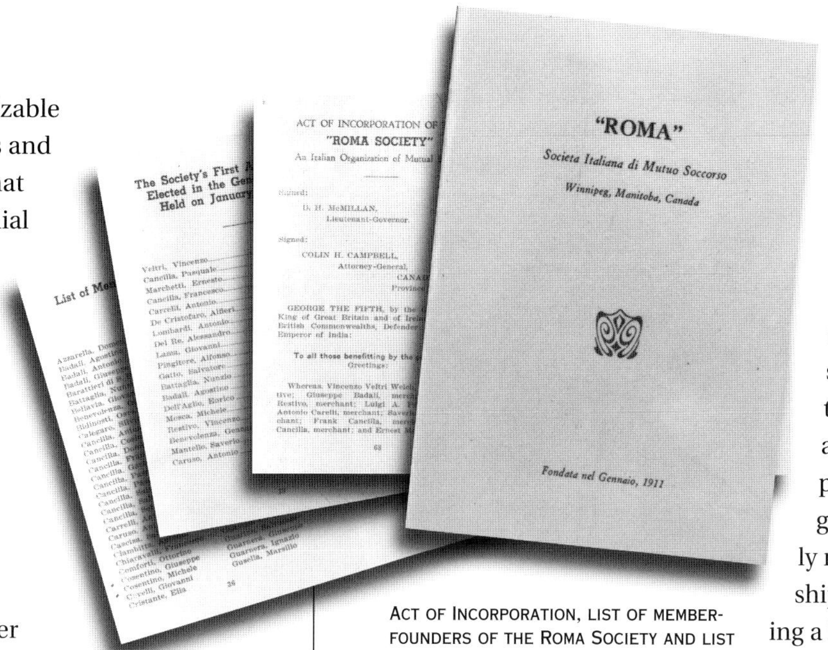

ACT OF INCORPORATION, LIST OF MEMBER-FOUNDERS OF THE ROMA SOCIETY AND LIST OF THE SOCIETY'S FIRST ADMINISTRATION, 1911. (AUGUST COSENTINO)

The Roma Society was a synthesis of a multitude of relationships–family, friendship, class, interdependence between petty entrepreneurs and workers, and regional ties–all woven together under the general rubric of mutual aid. In addition to offering financial benefits to its members in the case of sickness and death, the Roma Society also provided a sense of companionship and a forum for expressing one's concerns and dilemmas. For its leaders–the *prominenti*–the Roma Society was a vehicle for enhancing their business interests and strengthening their roles as intermediaries between newly arrived Italians and the representatives of Canadian political and civil society.

The most important institution in the early years of Winnipeg Italian history and the principal catalyst in the organizational life of the community was the Holy Rosary Church which opened its doors in October of 1923. Prior to 1912 many Winnipeg Italians worshipped at St. Mary's Cathedral. In 1911, Father Ferdinand Anzalone, a Sicilian, congregated a few Italian families at Sacre-Coeur. The following year he rented a small building in the West End where he conducted his masses. Anzalone left Winnipeg in 1915 to serve as chaplain in the Italian army, and between 1915 and 1923 no Italian pastors were sent to continue his work. During that time many of Anzalone's congregation attended the Church of the Immaculate Conception. At some point in this interval (no dates are available) the community's *prominenti* conducted a campaign to establish a church for the community. The entrepreneur Giuseppe Badali served as president of a fundraising committee which in due time was able to collect $25,000. With this money, the former Icelandic Church at the corner of Sherbrook and Bannatyne (near Little Italy) was purchased. At the opening ceremony, the Rev. A. A. Sinnott, Archbishop of Winnipeg, dedicated the Church of the Most Holy Rosary, and the Rev. Pietro Giletti was appointed pastor.

In addition to its spiritual role, Holy Rosary Church, throughout the years, sponsored non-religious initiatives such as folk dancing and music, theatre productions, and language courses, activities that would later be transferred to organizations of a secular nature.

HOLY ROSARY CHURCH, SHERBROOK AND BANNATYNE, WINNIPEG, 1929

The creation of a parish that would administer to the "spiritual needs" of Italians abroad was linked to the official policy of the Roman Catholic Church to expand the tenets of Catholicism to lands that were prevalently Protestant in nature, and to combat the rise of political philosophies that espoused militant social action and atheism, of which socialism was expressly singled out.

Church committees and organizations were an amalgam of religious belief and secular values. While the Church hierarchy viewed them as instruments for the dissemination of Catholic orthodoxy, Winnipeg Italians brought to them a constellation of roles, experiences, and values that often resulted in elaborate and complex entities that went beyond the need to attend to spiritual matters to address the exigencies of everyday life. Church life became another means by which familial traditions, kin relations, ties based on region of origin, and social class identities could be forged and solidified. The petty bourgeoisie, for example, viewed involvement in church activities as enhancing their prestige and expanding their contacts with Italians and the "host" society, factors that would ultimately serve their economic interests.

HOLY ROSARY CHURCH LADIES COMMITTEE, WINNIPEG, 1930S. (HOLY ROSARY CHURCH ARCHIVES)

During World War II, many Winnipeg Italian organizations were ordered by the Canadian government to suspend their activities. Roma Society meetings were declared illegal, while Italian language classes administered under the auspices of the Holy Rosary Church were abruptly terminated. Organizations that demonstrated fervent support for the Canadian war effort, such as the Holy Rosary Young People's Club, were allowed to carry on.

The crisis of the war years left its stains on the fabric of Italian-Canadian life. Kenneth Bagnell wrote unsparingly of the "confusion, discouragement and resentment"[3] that beset Italians and particularly the youth, who distanced themselves from their cultural origins. The re-activation of Italian organizations was left to those who were still willing to assert their ancestral identity in an unfavourable social climate, and to the new wave of immigrants unaware of the macabre events of the war and desirous of maintaining their cultural traditions.

The only new organization to emerge in Winnipeg immediately after the war was the Fratellanza Amatese. Essentially a mutual-aid society, its membership was open to individuals of Amatese background. In addition, the Holy Rosary Church and Roma Society cautiously picked up the pieces of their shattered foundations and began the earnest task of reconstituting themselves.

It took at least 10 years for Winnipeg Italians to mend the sense of belonging that the war years had shredded. The emergence of organizations such as the Leonardo DaVinci Society, the Fogolar Furlan (created by Friulani immigrants), and the Italo-Canadian Club, along with the establishment of an Italian radio program under the auspices of the Holy Rosary Church, suggests that only a flurry of activity could dissipate the agonies of the past.

THE HOLY ROSARY CHURCH YOUNG PEOPLE'S CLUB DANCE "LA TARANTELLA." 1939.

THE HOLY ROSARY CHURCH HOCKEY TEAM, C. 1941. (MANITOBA SPORTS HALL OF FAME & MUSEUM)

In 1963, the Holy Rosary Church spearheaded the creation of the Holy Rosary Italian Credit Union. This institution later severed its ties with the Church and was renamed the Italia Credit Union. As a community-based initiative it terminated its operations in the early 1980s.

In 1964, the existing associations, with the decisive input of the consular agent GiovanBattista Mottola and Holy Rosary Church pastor Father Domenico Fiore, and in consultation with Dr. Sam Loschiavo, formed the Italian Canadian League of Manitoba. The League was mandated to coordinate the activities of the various associations, foster the promotion of the Italian language and culture, and represent the "Italian community" at all levels of Canadian political and civil society.

While to the larger society the League was seen as an "ethnic association," its internal makeup was much more complex. The League was an amalgam of working-class and petty bourgeois elements, some of which had been forged in Canadian social reality while others were products of the social relations of Fascist and post-Fascist Italy, stamped with the nuances of regional variations.

PRESENTATION OF THE LEONARDO DAVINCI SOCIETY BURSARIES TO ITALIAN CANADIAN STUDENTS, WINNIPEG, 1956. FOREGROUND: ARTHUR V. MAURO. (HOLY ROSARY CHURCH ARCHIVES)

By the late 1960s, secular-based Italian organizations were predominant. In addition to the League and the already existing Leonardo DaVinci Society, a local chapter of the Dante Alighieri Cultural Society was formed in 1966, its membership consisting largely of academics and business people. The "Dante" organized Italian language classes, lectures on Italian history and culture, music recitals, and other activities.

In subsequent years, organizations named after regions and towns began to flourish. These were the Bari Club, Club Silano (province of Cosenza), the San Mango D'Aquino Society (province of Catanzaro), and the Club Siciliano di Winnipeg. Other organizations to emerge were the Italian Students Youth Association, the Italian Women's Association, the Sons of Italy (with male and female lodges), and various sports clubs.

In 1979, the League embarked on a campaign to raise funds towards the purchase of a building that would serve as a cultural centre. In 1980, it took possession of a building that had once been a credit union, remodelled it, and opened it to the public with the not-so-original name of Casa d'Italia. In the early 1980s, the Italian Women's Association, with the assistance of a group of professional and business people and the support of the Holy Rosary Church, began to promote the concept of a senior citizens' residence that would primarily serve "Canadians of Italian origin." This resulted in the creation of the Villa Cabrini Seniors' Residence, which began operating in 1985. The residence was named after St. Frances Xavier Cabrini, the patron saint of Italian immigrants.

CULTURAL DISPLAY ORGANIZED BY THE DANTE ALIGHIERI SOCIETY OF WINNIPEG, C. 1968. (HOLY ROSARY CHURCH ARCHIVES)

In the late 1980s, plans began for the development of a new and larger cultural centre that would replace the Casa d'Italia. This work culminated in the opening of the Centro Caboto in south Winnipeg in 1998.

In the late 1960s and early 1970s, two short-lived newspapers, *Il Messaggero Italo-Canadese* under the editorship of Franco Gotti, and *Il Progresso*, presented their readers with news from Italy, Canadian events, and information on the activities of local Italian organizations. A monthly newsmagazine entitled *Umanitas*,which sought to elevate the quality and breadth of intellectual discourse appeared in 1970. It never attracted a large reading audience, and within a year it ceased publication. Subsequent publications included *Per Conoscerci Meglio*, a monthly newsmagazine produced by the Club Siciliano, the *Casa d'Italia Bollettino*(bulletin), and *Il Giornale Italiano del Manitoba*, all of which were short-lived endeavours.

NOTES

1. Bruno Ramirez, "The Italians of Montreal: From Sojourning to Settlement, 1900–1921," in *Little Italies in North America*, ed.Betty Boyd Caroli, Robert F.Harney, and Lydio F. Tomasi (Toronto: Multicultural History Society of Ontario, 1978), p. 75.
2. Antonella Fanella, "Family, Honour and Destiny: Southern Italian Immigrants in Calgary, 1910–1990," (M.A. thesis, University of Calgary, 1991).
3. Kenneth Bagnell, *Canadese: A Portrait of the Italian Canadians* (Toronto: MacMillan, 1989), p. 96.

L I F E S T O R I E S

SAM FABRO *grew up in Winnipeg's "Little Italy" in the 1930s and 1940s. He later became a successful athlete and businessman. He remembers life in the Italian community in that period.*

It seemed that in those days family and kin had more time for each other. Each Sunday was spent visiting one another. On other occasions we would partake in the "Italian picnics" sponsored by the Holy Rosary Church, or get together at the Lido Plage which was run by an Italian family named Nesti. Another favourite pastime was to play musical instruments. We Fabros were musicians as well, and with time had developed a band. Bill was on saxophone, Dick on clarinet, Wally on trumpet–and I kept time.

SAM FABRO AT HIS INDUCTION TO THE MANITOBA HOCKEY HALL OF FAME, WINNIPEG, 1992. (SAM FABRO)

We had six Fabro cousins who lived about a quarter of a mile away. They would often join us to play street games which in those days were frowned upon by the law. One Sunday afternoon we were playing baseball when a policeman in a cruiser showed up and stopped the game. One by one we were asked our names and when the officer recorded the fifth Fabro name he started to laugh and proceeded to fold up his book.

At a young age I learned to play hockey on the Sherburn Rink (on the corner of Portage and Sherburn). Sherburn Rink consisted of three hockey rinks and a huge public skating rink; at times hundreds of people would join in the fun. At 30 or 40 degrees below zero you would freeze your toes off. Often we would run into the building to thaw out and then go out again and freeze all over again.

Prior to World War II and for a few short years after the war, the Catholic Hockey League became well known throughout Winnipeg. Triple-header games took place at the old Olympic Rink in the North End, often to capacity crowds. I played for Holy Rosary Church and was on two cup-winners in the late 1940s. At the time Father Borelli was Holy Rosary's parish priest. He took an active role in the development of the team. In between periods, he would often do the rosary.

JOHN BATTISTA *and* **MARIA FRANCESCA AIELLO** *tried to maintain some aspects of rural life in the middle of Winnipeg. Their story is told by their daughter Diana Nixon.*

Battista, my father, was among the very few who kept pigeons, chickens, and rabbits in his backyard. This ensured that the family would always have fresh eggs and fowl all of the time. The neighbourhood boys and girls were often attracted to Battista's backyard because of the animals.

Battista was a giving person and had a reputation for helping others in need by lending his hand in carpentry or gardening. He was an avid gardener and maintained four good-sized garden plots and a small vineyard.

Battista and Maria sponsored many relatives in coming to Canada in the 1950s, and opened their home to recent immigrants. The majority of them were family men who had left their loved ones behind. Although many of these men were lonely, Battista and Maria's house–241 Bartlett Avenue–became a home away from home. There were very few Sundays that one would not find two or three men spending the day and having dinner at Battista and Maria's house.

ALFONSINA *and* **GEREMINO CORDILEONE** *raised their family in the 1930s and 1940s among neighbours who often did not understand their customs. Their story is told my their daughter, Josephine Dellapenta.*

Life was hard. They lived in a culture which was alien to their way of life. For example, Alfonsina had a wood stove in the garage. In that same garage, every year she made her tomato sauce and she preserved fruits and vegetables. The Cordileones also made their own wine; they made sure the grapes came at night when it was dark so that the neighbours wouldn't see what they were doing. They were afraid of what the neighbours might say or think. To "eliminate the evidence" the cases which contained the grapes were burned in the furnace. The neighbours would often call the Cordileones "wops" or "dagos," or would often refer to them as "those Italians."

The Cordileones also struggled through the Great Depression. In order to make ends meet they rented rooms in their house. Alfonsina kept her family fed as she knew how to make a lot with very little at hand.

There were, of course, good times. Sundays were wonderful; they were family days. Alfonsina and Jimmy arose before the rest of the family and went to the kitchen where they would have their coffee. Then, Alfonsina would make the sauce. The family always woke up to the smell of frying meatballs and sauce cooking on the stove; it was wonderful! The family would attend Mass and return home to enjoy the main meal of the day–spaghetti. Often our grandparents would visit, or we would visit them, and then go to see other friends.

GEREMINO AND ALFONSINA CORDILEONE ON THEIR WEDDING DAY, WINNIPEG, 1926. (JOSEPHINE DELLAPENTA NÉE CORDILEONE).

Some Sundays we would take a streetcar to the city park or pile into the back of a friend's truck and go on a picnic out to St. Charles or Lockport. On other occasions we would go to the beach.

Christmas and Easter were special occasions. Christmas Eve dinner was very special, with fish dishes, anchovy-fried bread, and other goodies. Christmas dinner consisted of homemade spaghetti in soup, turkey, roast potatoes, vegetables, salad, lupini, sausages, wine, bowls of assorted fruits, and chestnuts, mixed nuts, topped off with traditional fruit cake, which Alfonsina had learned to make.

UMBERTO *and* **FILOMENA CURATOLO** *came to Winnipeg in the 1950s. They settled in Winnipeg's multi-ethnic North End, where they formed bonds with neighbours from many other cultures. Their story is told by their daughter Teresa Campanelli.*

In 1958, when my parents found out that family members from Italy were coming to live in Winnipeg, they decided to become homeowners. They purchased a three-storey house for $11,000 on Pritchard Avenue (in the North End). The house was owned at the time by the Baclers, a Polish family who had saved enough money to move to a better home.

The Baclers had a tenant by the name of Angela Benczarsky.

Angela was a widow who had lived in the house for many years. Angela asked if she could continue to stay in the house. My parents agreed to have her stay on as a tenant. Angela became the grandmother figure who helped introduce my mother to the ways of life in Winnipeg. She introduced our family to toast, macaroni and cheese, and mayonnaise.

With a small down payment, a kind tenant, and the Baclers to carry the mortgage, my parents were proud of their accomplishments. Now they were able to welcome their family members and give them a place to stay.

By the end of 1960, their second daughter was born, and all three storeys of the house were filled with three families, and Angela Benczarsky.

Living on Pritchard Avenue meant having a variety of ethnic neighbours: Polish, Jewish, Ukrainian, and German. In their broken English and diverse accents, the neighbours established respectable friendships. Though they never socialized in their homes, they always found time to chit-chat in their front or backyards.

Being one of the few Italian families to live in the North End was a unique experience. Shopping was done mainly on Selkirk Avenue–at Oretzki's, Misha Pollack's, Clifford's, and Tom Boy's. When the Palettas opened up their grocery store on Notre Dame, my parents did most of their shopping there. Mrs. Paletta always cut their meat just right, and Mr. Paletta delivered the groceries and drove the customers right to their homes. If there wasn't enough money one week to pay the groceries, the Palettas would put them on the tab until the following week.

Our family seemed to adjust well to life in Winnipeg, and in 1962 a third child–a son–was born.

During this time, my father Umberto continued to do construction work (plasterer and bricklayer) and Filomena quit her job to raise the children. The families that had come from Italy had jobs in sewing factories and had made enough money to purchase their own homes. My parents had no choice but to rent out two of the three storeys. It was difficult having non-Italian tenants. The rapport just wasn't the same as it was with family. The sense of being secure in your own home was greatly diminished. Yet they had no choice; rental payments helped them to pay their bills.

Our family began to socialize more, especially with other Italians. It attended functions sponsored by the Holy Rosary Church, Italian picnics, and special occasions such as when a singer from Italy (Claudio Villa, for example) came to town. During this time there wasn't enough money to purchase a vehicle, so a bus was used, unless it was a special occasion, and then a taxicab was called.

ALBUM
Images of Winnipeg Italians

Da restituirsi alla fine del viaggio alle persone incaricate del ritiro del biglietto.

Al Passeggiere № 034510 *

NAVIGAZIONE GENERALE ITALIANA

SOCIETÀ RIUNITE FLORIO, RUBATTINO E LLOYD ITALIANO

SOCIETÀ ANONIMA SEDE IN GENOVA

Biglietto di SECONDA CLASSE Economica N. [redacted]

RILASCIATO ALLE CONDIZIONI INDICATE A TERGO

DA GENOVA A NEW YORK

COL P.FO ROMA

PER N.° 2 POST... A FAVORE DE... SIGNOR — PARTENZA DEL 3 MAG. 1929

	ETÀ	POSTI
1		
2		
3		
4		
5		

CABIN 369 – 367

LETT C – F

TOTALE POSTI 2

GENOVA LI 3 MAG. 1929

NAVIGAZIONE GENERALE ITALIANA

AGRICULTURAL WORKERS IN CALABRIA, ITALY C. 1910 (COLLEZIONE PANZARELLA, CURINGA)
STEAMSHIP TICKET ISSUED TO ACHILLE TOROSSI, 1929.

School children in the town of Grimaldi (c. 1929) one of the many small towns which sent immigrants to Winnipeg (Emilio Anselmo)

INSIDE THE OLYMPIA CAFE (C. 1913) OWNED BY THE BADALI FAMILY, WHO WERE AMONG THE EARLIEST ITALIAN IMMIGRANTS TO WINNIPEG (SENA BADALI)

THE WEDDING PARTIES OF SEVERAL EARLY WINNIPEG ITALIAN FAMILIES: (OPPOSITE) FRANK POLTRONETTI AND MARY MIGNACCA (1929), (ABOVE LEFT) NICKY DELLAPENTA AND JOSIE FRANCISCONE (1922) AND (ABOVE RIGHT) SAM CASCISA AND JENNY DERCOLA (1936).

The Sellan family c. 1930s (Marilouise Lisi) and the Aiello family, 1926 (Diana Nixon)

Above: The Cantafio family, 1940s (Lucy Mottola). Right: Tony and Peter Sherbo (sons of Arcangelo and Maria Sherbo), Catanzaro, Italy, 1926 (Charles Sherbo)

ROSARIO SANFILIPO AND SALVATORE SCALETTA, SICILIAN FRUIT PEDDLARS, WINNIPEG, 1929 (IGNATIUS SCALETTA)

THE OLYMPIA CAFE, 1913 (SENA BADALI)

Very successful Dance
Net Profit $57.45

Oct. 21/24

DANCE
WILL BE GIVEN BY
The ITALIAN GIRLS CLUB
IN
THE COLUMBUS HALL
CORNER SMITH & GRAHAM STS.
ON
TUESDAY, OCTOBER 21ST 1924
AT 8.30 P.M.
TICKETS 50 CENTS

Feb. 24/25

THE ITALIAN GIRLS CLUB
DANCE
AT THE
NORMAN HALL
SHERBROOKE ST.
TUESDAY FEBRUARY 24, 1925
Snappy Music
50 Cents
Tickets

Receipts $103.50
Expenses 68.50
Profit $ 35.00.

SOME OF THE DIFFERENT COMMUNITY ORGANIZATIONS: RECORDS FROM THE ITALIAN GIRLS CLUB (ABOVE); THE ROMA SOCIETY PICNIC, 1925 (TOP RIGHT); THE HOLY ROSARY CHURCH YOUTH CLUB, 1939 (RIGHT)

LEFT: THE IACHETTA FAMILY, 1946 (EMILIO ANSELMO). ABOVE: THE DERCOLA FAMILY AND KIN AT THE COTTAGE, C. 1930S (JENNY CASCISA)

LEFT: LORETTA LISI (POLTRONETTI) ON HER BIRTHDAY, 1937 (MARILOUISE LISI). ABOVE: THE DEL BIGIO FAMILY AT RANCHO DON CARLOS, C. 1956 (PHIL DEL BIGIO)

Carol Mottola,
Corydon Avenue c. 1955.
Above: Grimaldesi immigrants in Winnipeg, 1952
(Emilio Anselmo)

ABOVE: MEMORIAL MASS FOR PARISH MEMBERS WHO DIED IN WORLD WAR II, 1946
AT THE FIRST HOLY ROSARY CHURCH

BELOW: INSIDE THE FIRST HOLY ROSARY CHURCH, 1937
(SHERBROOK AND BANNATYNE)

HOLY ROSARY CHURCH CONFIRMATION AND FIRST COMMUNION CLASSES, 1968

First Confirmation & Communion Classes in the New Church

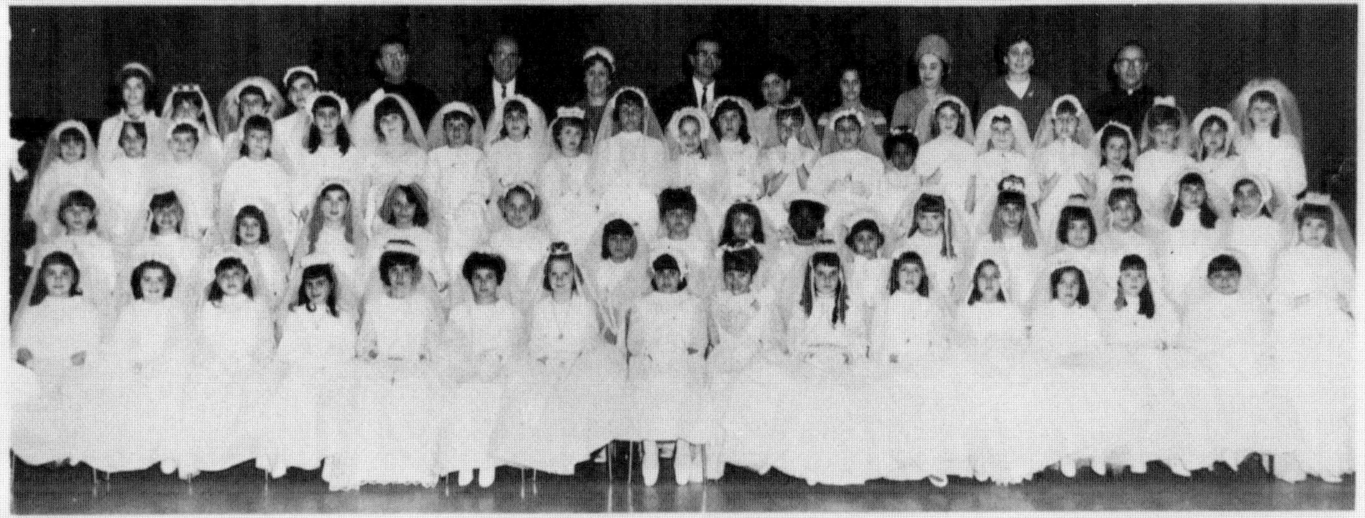

May 19, 1968 Communion   Confirmation May 24, 1968

May 19, 1968   Confirmation 24, 1968

Italian folk dancers and singers, Walker Theatre, 1928 (Holy Rosary Church Archives)

ITALIAN FOLK DANCERS AND SINGERS, ASSINIBOINE PARK, 1931 (HOLY ROSARY CHURCH ARCHIVES)

"OTELLO O IL MORO DI VENEZIA"
Dramma in 5 Atti Di
Guglielmo Shakespeare
Rappresentato Dalla Compagnia Filodrammatica Italiana
Nella Sala Del S. Cuore—Winnipeg, Man.
McDermot e Lydia Sts.
Domenica 7 Dicembre, 1930

OTELLO, moro al servizio di Venezia	J. Bellon
DOGE DI VENEZIA	P. R. Bidinost
BRABANZIO, padre di Desdemona	J. Mottola
LUDOVICO, congiunto di Brabanzio	S. Mascarin
CASSIO, luogotenente di Otello	A. Bellon
IAGO, alfiere di Otello	A. Scinocca
MONTANO, governatore di Cipro	C. Mainella
RODRIGO, gentiluomo veneto	E. Morelli
DESDEMONA, moglie di Otello	M. Amantea
EMILIA, moglie di Iago	E. Chiarot
PRIMO UFFICIALE	P. Perin
SECONDO UFFICIALE	E. Battiston

THE HOLY ROSARY CHURCH THEATRE GROUP PRODUCTION OF "OTHELLO," 1930 (HOLY ROSARY CHURCH ARCHIVES)

ITALIAN FLOAT AT DOMINION DAY PARADE, 1927 (HOLY ROSARY CHURCH ARCHIVES)

ITALIAN FLOAT DURING WINNIPEG'S DIAMOND JUBILEE, 1949 (HOLY ROSARY CHURCH ARCHIVES)

The Fratellanza Amatese (shown here at their 1951 social evening) were one of several groups that united pre-war and post-war Italian immigrants (Lucy Mottola)

IMAGES OF WINNIPEG ITALIANS IN THE LATE 1950S AND EARLY 1960S. OPPOSITE (LEFT TO RIGHT): THE FIORENTINO AND CIANFLONE FAMILIES AND FRIENDS, 1961 (CONNIE FIORENTINO-SHERBO); TARCISIO MARDERO IN FRONT OF THE LEGISLATIVE BUILDING, 1957; THE VISIT OF ITALIAN SINGER LUCIANO TAJOLI IN 1962; MAMMA TROSSI (1962) OWNER OF THE POPULAR MAMMA TROSSI'S RISTORANTE. ABOVE: THE HOLY ROSARY CHURCH YOUTH GROUP'S JAZZ CABARET (1963) AND AN ADVERTISEMENT FOR THE VISIT OF ITALIAN SINGER CLAUDIO VILLA (1965)

The Italia Soccer team, 1955-56 (Holy Rosary Church Archives)

The Holy Rosary Church Baseball team, 1949-51

THE HOLY ROSARY CHURCH YOUTH GROUP, 1964

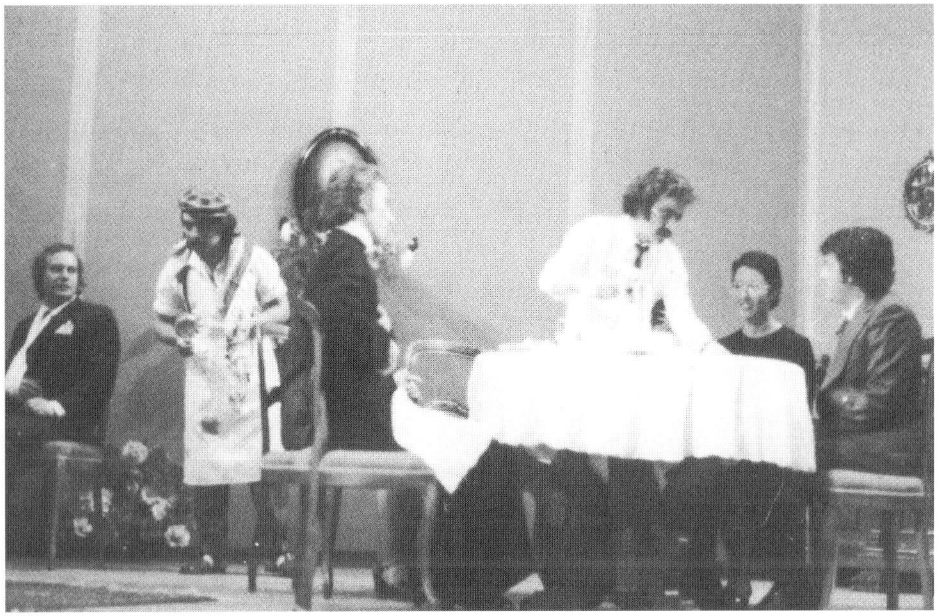

"GLI AMICI DEL TEATRO" (1972)
ITALIAN LANGUAGE CLASS (LUISA CARBONE, INSTRUCTOR), 1961
(HOLY ROSARY CHURCH ARCHIVES)

APPENDIX

The North Italy Farmers Colony

While most Italian immigrants to Manitoba came to Winnipeg or other urban centres, in the 1920s there was one short-lived effort to develop an agricultural settlement of Italians in rural Manitoba. In 1921, a Winnipeg Italian by the name of Joseph Ghezzi placed an advertisement in the Milan newspaper *Il Mercato Universale* encouraging Italians to settle in Manitoba. This advertisement came to the attention of British officials in Italy. According to their investigation, Ghezzi claimed to have received a grant of about 50 square miles (supposedly from the Canadian government) in southern Manitoba which he wished to colonize with agriculturalists from the Lombardy region of Italy. Ghezzi also contended that the Italian government, through its representative in Winnipeg—the vice consul Count Giuseppi Barattieri—showed great interest in this scheme. The community that Ghezzi planned to establish would be called the North Italian Farmers Colony.

Eventually, this plan came to the attention of Winston Churchill, then Secretary of State for the Colonies. In reply to his inquiries, Governor-General Lord Byng of Vimy, stated that the Canadian government did not endorse the Societá Italo-Canadese, nor had it granted Ghezzi the 50 square miles of land.

There is some evidence that Mussolini's regime tried—unsuccesfully—to use the Farmers Colony as part of its plans to promote Fascism among Italian-Canadian communities. In 1923 Italia Garibaldi, granddaughter of Giuseppe Garibaldi, visited Canada to "promote an Italian agricultural colonization scheme in Manitoba." During her stay in Winnipeg, she met with Manitoba Premier John Bracken, Joseph Ghezzi, and others to discuss the viability of establishing an Italian farm colony in southern Manitoba. While Garibaldi was in Canada promoting the colonization scheme, she was also able to organize Fascist locals in Toronto, Winnipeg and Montreal.[1]

Within two years of Garibaldi's visit, an agrarian settlement made up largely of northern Italians had been established at Lorette, Manitoba. In 1925 it was incorporated by a provincial order-in-council under the name of the North Italy Farmers Colony Limited. In the articles of incorporation, Ghezzi is identified as the manager. In addition to its holdings at Lorette, the colony purchased blocks of land outside of Alonsa, and in the Glenella district.

In its brief history, the colony functioned as a cooperative venture, whereby each individual deposited a minimum of $200 and in return would work for the colony and be given room and board, clothing, and money for expenses. At the end of the year, 50 percent of the profits would be distributed among the colonists, while the other 50 percent was put into a reserve fund.

By 1928, it seems that the Colony was no longer financially viable. With the dissolution of its operations, some of the colonists took up residence in Winnipeg, while others may have settled in other parts of Canada, or returned to Italy.

While managing the colony, Ghezzi was also Managing Director of Luigi Calissano and figli, Wine Merchants and Importers, with office and warehouse located on the corner of Graham and Vaughan in Winnipeg. In the Henderson Directory for the year 1931 Ghezzi is listed as a clerk. His name is absent from the 1932 Directory, never to reappear.

NOTES

1. John Zucchi, *Italians in Toronto*, p. 171.

DOCUMENTS OF THE NORTH ITALY FARMERS COLONY

To J.H. Henderson, Commercial Secretary in the British Embassy, Rome, from H.W. Kennard.

Rome, 17 November 1921.

I have the honour to report that my attention was called to an advertisement which appeared in "Il Mattino" of October 25th, and in other papers, of which the following is a translation.

> Unemployed, demobilised pensioners, industrials, agricultural labourers, workers in all professions, arts and crafts, desirous to go abroad alone or with family find occupation immediately, rich future, by applying to great English colonial society (Italian Branch). Healthy resort, Government concessions free of charge, vast lands, machinery, animals, lodgings, immense gain. Information free by applying to the Commissario Post Box 352 Milan 4251

Several enquirers called at the Embassy asking for particulars, one of whom had answered the advertisement and had received a reply from "Il Mercato Universale", a newspaper in Milan, a reply consisting of a printed unsigned circular, and a copy of the newspaper containing a notice of the scheme. These I sent to the Canadian Trade Commissioner at Milan, asking if he could confirm a statement contained in the newspaper, to the effect that the Company had the support of the Canadian Government. He answered that neither he nor the Canadian Superintendent of Emigration in London, to whom he wrote, believed the statement to be true, and that the Canadian Government had been communicated with.

Mr. Churchill [Winston Churchill, then British Secretary of State for the Colonies] has sent me a report dated 10th November prepared by Mr. Vice Consul Swan after an interview with the Director of the "Mercato Universale." From this it appears that the "Societh [sic] Italo-Canadese" is composed of Signor J. Ghezzi, P.O.Box 2938, Winnipeg; Mr. J.O. Dubce, of the firm of J.A. Herbert Courtiers, 265 Avenue du Fertage [Portage], Winnipeg; and Mr. Al. Bernier, M.P. of Bernier, Blackwood and Bernier, Solicitors of Winnipeg.

Signor Ghezzi, an Italian who has made a great deal of money, has received a grant of about 50 square miles of land in Manitoba, and wishes to colonise it with a hundred Lombardy families of agriculturalists, who must pay their own fare to Canada and supply their own funds.

The Canadian Government support is apparently the land grant, the Italian government support, which is also claimed in the advertisement, is presumably the interest of Conte Barattieri, the Italian Consul at Winnipeg, who is seemingly a friend of Ghezzi and takes an interest in the scheme.

The "Mercato Universale" were requested to publish in the Italian press the advertisement prepared by Ghezzi, receive the replies and give all necessary information.

At the expense of the "Societh [sic] Italo-Canadese" and "Mercato Universale" have published a pamphlet entitled "Canada West-Western Canada", containing translated extracts from the Canadian Immigration Regulations, taken from the official "Canada West" published by the Canadian Immigration Ministry.

Some eight hundred replies have been received to the various departments, but most applicants have withdrawn when informed that they must pay their own passage to Canada.

Mr. Swan was of the opinion that the Director of "Il Mercato Universale" was acting in good faith, and merely as the paid agent of the Canadian principals, but did not appear to him that the scheme was sound or sufficiently guaranteed. He saw letters on headed note paper from Messrs. Herbert & and Co. regarding the scheme, which referred to Mr. Bernier and Signor Ghezzi, but he saw no communication from Signor Ghezzi himself.

Count Barattieri, who is in Italy on leave, is stated to have called at the offices of "Il Mercato Universale" a short while ago, when he gave a good report of Ghezzi and the scheme.

(National Archives of Canada)

To Winston Churchill, British Secretary of State for the Colonies from Lord Byng of Vimy, Governor-General of Canada

Ottawa, 30 December 1921

With reference to your dispatch No. 675 of the 29th November last, regarding a scheme for settling Italian emigrants in Manitoba, I have the honour to inform you that the Immigration Department reports that investigation at Winnipeg, which is the headquarters of the Societh [sic] Italo-Canadese, shows that there is a Society formed or in process of formation there whose President is Mr. J. Ghezzi, a manufacturer, and whose Secretary is Mr. J. O. Dubce. The President admits having written to Italy informing the Mercato Universale of the proposition to encourage the settlement of Italians in Manitoba but says that he did not authorize publicity in Italy and apparently declines to accept any responsibility. So far as the Department of Immigration (the Department through which naturally any encouragement would be given to the scheme) is concerned, no such encouragement has been given by the Canadian government either by the granting of land or in any other way. The Department of Immigration further is not aware that the persons in Winnipeg are in a position to operate successfully any land or settlement scheme.

Memorandum to file from F. C. Blair, Department of Immigration and Colonization

Ottawa, 6 Februry 1923

Miss Garibaldi called at the Office this morning and as she is about to return to Italy, decided to leave with the Department a general memorandum covering her visit and her observations.

(1) Miss Garibaldi arrived in Canada on the 4th December and expects to sail from St. John on the 10th instant. During this period Miss Garibaldi has visited the Federal Government in Ottawa and the Provincial Governments at Winnipeg, Regina and districts, Montreal, the mining districts of Northern Ontario, Toronto, and various points in the Western Provinces, not including British Columbia.

(2) Miss Garibaldi visited Edmonton and Calgary. At Edmonton she had an interview with the Hon. George Headley, Minister of Agriculture, who expressed his interest in the immigration of Italian farmers. Miss Garibaldi saw a co-operative Italian mine and sawmill in operation at a point north of Edmonton. At Calgary she spoke to the Business Men's Club and at the close, had laid before her an irrigation scheme. Nothing definite came out of that but Miss Garibaldi secured information as to the location and price of irrigated land.

(3) Miss Garibaldi stayed two days at the Lt. Governor's home in Regina. She went to the Parliament Buildings and there saw Mr. Dunning, the Premier, who gladly left his Office and took her to see an Italian Colony. She found these people doing very well and the Hon. Mr. Dunning gave her a special map and told her where this land was located. She spoke before the Canadian Club and the Daughters of the Empire who were very interested in her work and stated if any Italian immigrants came out they would do what they could to assist them and would even supply them with music boxes, which Miss Garibaldi states will win their hearts.

(4) From Regina Miss Garibaldi went to Winnipeg where she saw Hon. Mr. Bracken. With him Miss Garibaldi went to the Parliament House and there met four Mennonite leaders with Mr. Black their lawyer, and an Italian by the name of Ghezzi. These Mennonites are from southern Manitoba and they told Miss Garibaldi that they were leaving Canada for Mexico. They stated that the area of land they own in Manitoba is sufficient for 20,000 people. They desire to leave the land as soon as arrangements can be made for the sale of this land. They made a proposal that the Italian government select from northern Italy a large number of Italians and send them out to these lands in southern Manitoba. It was proposed that some scheme of financial assistance be rendered the Italian government. They are asking $30.00 an acre for the unseeded land and $32.00 an acre if the land is seeded. This amount would include the improvements and they would accept a reasonable figure for their farm stock and implements. If the Italian government will guarantee to refund the money a group of financial men will undertake the responsibility. The proposal is that the Italian government will make the selection of settlers and that if they have any money they will pay it to the Italian government before they leave in order to re-imburse the Italian government for their support. When these men arrive and take up the land they will continue their payments to the Italian government and the Italian government will deal with this group of financial men. They will pay interest at 6%.

(5) Miss Garibaldi is leaving tonight to go to Quebec where she will see Mr. Richard.

(Provincial Archives of Manitoba)

Excerpt from a memorandum from Thomas Gelley, Division Commissioner of Immigration to W.J. Egan, Deputy Minister of Immigration

Ottawa, 9 September 1926

With reference to the North Italy Farmers Association at Lorette, I may state that I recently paid a visit to this colony and found that the whole personnel there was working on this farm or for other farms in the vicinity. Besides operating their farms at Lorette and a cheese factory which the Italians have opened lately, at that point, these Italians are also operating another large farm a few miles east of Winnipeg. There are at present seven families on the farm at Lorette, besides twenty-eight single men. The colony possesses over 100 head of cattle, 100 head of horses, hogs, etc.

There are over fifty Italians who came forward this year now operating 44 quarter sections of land northwest of Portage la Prairie at Alonsa, Manitoba. They have put into crop this year on these farms over 1200 acres of land, which would not have been under cultivation otherwise. They have summerfallowed on the same land over 2000 acres, besides breaking a large acreage of new land.

The Italians are good workers and many of the farmers who have seen them at work are well satisfied with their services and this is the reason why they are making application for them. I hope you will agree with me that it is fair to encourage and help this kind of immigration. There are many Italian farmers too, who are encouraging their countrymen to go to farming.

I may also state that a large percentage of Italians who came forward this year are at farm work in this district, and that the percentage of Italians actually at farm work who came forward this year is larger than any other nationality, either from preferred or non-preferred countries, with the exception of the Mennonites.

You may rest assured Mr. Egan, that there is no intention of wholesale admission of Italians contemplated, but I may state that it is expected that between now and February next quite a number of applications will be submitted for next year's employment. I will give all applications of this class my personal attention and will also endeavour to the best of my ability, to see that none but bona fide cases are accepted.

(Provincial Archives of Manitoba)

From Report of the Survey of Unused Lands in Manitoba written by R.W. Murchie and H.C. Grant for the Manitoba government in 1926

An interesting experiment in co-operative farming is found in the North Italy Farmers Colonies at Lorette and Alonsa. The members of this company are Italian farmers from the Lomellina district of North Italy who deposit a minimum of $200.00 each. The membership also includes Italians from this district already resident in Canada. The plan of operations is to purchase large blocks of partially developed land which are operated as units under a manager. All members are given work on the property and are paid standard wages, which they may leave wholly or partially with the company in order to build up their capital shares. If there is not enough work in the colony several members are released for work outside subject to recall at any time. As soon as the farms are sufficiently developed the families of the members will be brought out and established, but the co-operative basis will be maintained until the farms are fully paid for.

Last year the company operated 1,250 acres at Lorette and 8,000 acres at Alonsa, and had begun negotiations for the purchase of several thousand acres in Glenella district.

It is too early to pronounce on the value of the project, but the spirit of the colony is at present thoroughly co-operative and augurs well for success in that the capital of the company more than doubled in the 12-month period.

From The Tracks of Time: Glenella and Districts by the Glenella History Committee (1990)

In 1926 a group of men from Italy were interested in setting up an Italian commune or community in Manitoba, under the management of M. Ghezzi.

The first ten settlers each paid $200.00 to start this new venture. Others followed until there was an approximate total of one hundred.

The land was leased from the Great West Life Assurance Company with the intention of purchasing. The location of the land was in different areas, the largest being near Alonsa, Manitoba. Three quarter section was located in the Tupper area and three quarter section in the Glenella area. The former Bancroft house in Glenella, Manitoba was rented as headquarters and distribution point. Settlers came by train from Winnipeg to Glenella as well as repairs, merchandise, etc., and were transferred to the various locations.

William Martin of Glenella was hired at $60 per month as taxi man and dray man. The majority of horses were purchased from Fred Bullock and Wilmot Gill and were driven to locations where required. Twenty Holstein cows were shipped from Winnipeg to Glenella and were walked to the Alonsa area—a distance of eighteen miles.

By 1928 the financial situation became serious and operations closed down.

From Rainbow's End by the Kinosota-Alonsa District Historical Society (1985)

In 1926, a Commune Settlement was set up by a group of Italian settlers. The farms were not all in one block, but the main farm was the one now owned by John Sucharyna. Another was the N.J. Turko farm and still another the farm directly south of John Szymesko. Other quarters, belonging to the group, were located in the same general vicinity. One of the "Crowe houses" in Alonsa (the two-storey buildings, one of which is left and once occupied by Ellie Sul), was used as a business headquarters, where on Friday evenings, meetings of the Commune were held.

The main farm had large kitchens and a huge outdoor bake oven of stone and cement, for bread etc. The community had about one hundred men, most of whom were single.

A few settlers were families. On the farm south of Mrs. Mary Szymesko, the couple were known as Rena and Gula—surname forgotten. She often visited them and found them friendly, kindly neighbors. The settlement at first was supplied with barrels of wine . . . and the kindly Gula and Rena often presented Mrs. Szymesko with little pails full which they urged her to drink instead of water.

In May, they went out gathering the thimble-shaped black mushrooms. Later each morning, they gathered fresh dandelion leaves, they used like lettuce for salad. Chocolates were a favorite sweet.

Farming in Manitoba must have been much different than in Italy, and local people such as George Turko, and others were hired to work for them . . . The Italians only stayed about two and a half years. No doubt they found farming here an unprofitable operation. Authorities informed them the finances were all used and the settlers seemed to simply slip away . . . leaving their farms deserted.